THE GRAND BAZAAR

The Truth Behind the Wars in Iraq, Libya and Syria

ERIC PILON

CONTENTS

PROLOGUE

"If Barack Obama decides to attack the Syrian regime, he has ensured—for the very first time in history—that the United States will be on the same side as [Al-Qaeda]."

These wise words above were set down on paper in 2013 by the renowned journalist Robert Fisk, who had warned the former U.S. President of the danger of intervening militarily in the Syrian conflict, where meet a wide variety of radical groups that share at least one goal: to turn Syria into an Islamic state. Fisk was right on one point, but he was wrong on the other: it would not have been a first if United States soldiers had stood alongside members of Al-Qaeda on the field; far from it. We could pick the Kosovo Liberation Army (KLA) as a good example. Hailed by the Clinton administration and supported by the U.S. military, the KLA was mostly made up of Islamists, some of whom had spent time in Al-Qaeda camps in Afghanistan. Consider also the Taliban, with whom the Americans were in contact even though they knew that this Islamist faction was sheltering the Al-Qaeda high command, including Osama bin Laden. And let's not forget to mention that a few groups in Libya, as we will discover in this book, protected American diplomats in Benghazi while waving the flag of jihad. There's no doubt that the United States and its allies, especially the British, are partly responsible for the rise of Islamic fundamentalism in the

West if only because Washington and London, for purely economic reasons, have chosen to make common cause with the godmother of modern Islamism, Saudi Arabia, itself allied for several decades to the godfather of this totalitarian doctrine, the Muslim Brotherhood. The pockets stuffed with petrodollars, the Saudi princes, beginning in the 60s, financed the construction of mosques in Europe, Canada and the United States, where, even today, fundamentalist imams, most of them fresh out of Saudi and Egyptian universities, preach Wahhabism, the most puritanical branch of Islam. In parallel, for years the Saudis poured millions of dollars into the coffers of the Muslim Brotherhood that took the opportunity to create organizations that have become spearheads of Islamic lobbying in the West.

In Libya and Syria, the naivety—or foolishness—of Washington's political class became apparent in the earliest days of the Arab Spring when Barack Obama and his entourage joined forces with Qatar, Saudi Arabia and Turkey in a campaign to overthrow the regimes of Muammar Gaddafi and Bashar al-Assad. They teamed up with these states even though each of them proposes a political model that is diametrically opposite of the Western conception of democracy. It was therefore predictable that, both in Libya and Syria, these great standard-bearers of Islam would support dogmatic groups by offering them money and logistics so they could wage war against the Syrian troops, servants of a secular regime that Islamists of all stripes despise. Strange destiny: the Obama administration, on the one hand, wanted to overthrow a secular government that collaborated in the war against terrorism, while, on the other hand, it trusted Islamists to make this operation possible. When the Americans realized the mess this approach had left, it was already too late. History repeats itself: the Afghan, Kosovar, Iraqi, Libyan and Syrian conflicts represent, each in their way, further steps toward the complete Islamization of the Middle East. While Islamist countries continue to reject the precepts of the Enlightenment, the scions of this Enlightenment, the Western states, associate with them to protect their economic and geopolitical interests. The problem is that to protect its interests, a country must too often rely on weapons and go to war, or at least leave the dirty work to another country or private military companies, making sure to guide the precious allies as to the objectives they must pursue. This is pretty much what the United States has been doing since the end of the Second World War, and in most cases, the results have been catastrophic. Iraq, Libya, and Syria are a succession of failures in international diplomacy, which failures have shown that the situation will only improve when the Western world can finally free itself from the Islamic oil. But then, the road may be quite long.

This work is not a complete account of the Iraqi, Libyan, and Syrian conflicts. The goal here is to address the subject from a realistic viewpoint in an effort to set the records straight and debunk the myths related to each conflict, a task that can be fulfilled only if we agree to leave aside all fake news and conspiracy theories, which abound on the Internet and on bookstore shelves. In these times when propaganda has never been so intense, separating fact from fiction is a challenging mission. As such, the reader will notice that no ideological angle was favored. Three U.S. presidents had to contend with the Iraqi, Libyan and Syrian adventures; two Republicans and one Democrat, and all of them are to be blamed for the chaos that followed in Iraq, Libya, and Syria. If the author embraces some form of cynicism with regard to the political class—which is reflected in some of his remarks—, he nevertheless makes it a point of remaining ideologically neutral by avoiding to take a stance, even though this mission is only possible by exercising a certain restraint. The tone is far from the editorial, that is, it is not used for promotional hype purposes for one camp or the other—a reality that we see too often in many books—, but nor is it devoid of personal, moral judgment. As stated above, it is in the nature of the author to be cynical and he does not feel the need to justify himself to express opinions he describes as "rational." History will absolve him.

In fact, the serious flaws regarding the U.S. foreign policy have nothing to do with the Democratic or Republican labels. They rather relate to the country's dependence on oil. After all, the U.S.'s high standard of living is at stake, and here, the difficulty does not necessarily lie in a hypothetical breakdown of capitalism, but in what countries have done with the said capitalism, an economic system subjected to a geopolitical context responsible for the main conflicts of the last decades. Those of Iraq, Libya and Syria are no exception to this rule.

THE AMERICAN INTERVENTION IN IRAQ: THE CRIME OF THE CENTURY?

The war in Iraq is the failure of two administrations, of two presidents who were convinced, each on his side of the ideological spectrum, that their decisions were based on reason: the reason of state for George W. Bush, the reason based on the right of peoples to self-determination for Barack Obama. The first went down in history for having rid the world of Saddam Hussein, a bloodthirsty dictator, while the second, in a burst of "generosity", put Iraq back into the hands of Iraqis. Unfortunately, the simple observer can only paint an unflattering portrait of the Iraqi expedition, as its consequences were fatal. Documents published on the Wikileaks website show that between January 1, 2004, and December 31, 2009, the U.S. intervention in Iraq caused 109,032 deaths, including 66,081 civilians. Those already devastating figures do not take into account the number of fatalities from March 19, 2003, when the conflict started, to December 31 of the same year, anymore than they take into account the 1,200 civilians killed in at least two battles in Fallujah. And this tragic episode in the history of Iraq did not end on December 31, 2009. A civil war followed the withdrawal of the American troops in 2011, which led to the emergence of a group that would, for a time, terrorize the region and sweep almost everything away in its path: the Islamic State, or ISIS.

Why did the United States declare war on Iraq? To take possession of the country's oil reserves, some pseudo-experts said. Was that really the case? The Iraqi oil, it should be noted, belongs to Iraq, not to the United States. Before the 2003 intervention, Saddam Hussein's oil industry was running at full capacity, but the fall was rather brutal after the first sounds of the U.S. military's drums of war, the Iraqi state losing nearly half of its production. The United States subsequently had no choice but to comply with its obligation to authorize the new Iraqi government to sell its oil on the world market, just as it was doing before the conflict. But if the Americans did not intervene in Iraq to get hold of the country's oil, does this mean they did so because Saddam Hussein possessed weapons of mass destruction, which posed a danger to international security? Unlikely. Especially since the future showed that this rhetoric had been cooked up by the White House even though the CIA had made it clear that such weapons were nonexistent in Iraq. At first glance, then, there remains only one assumption: the U.S. intervention was justified by the fact that Baghdad had established relations with Al-Qaeda. After 9/11, the Americans, who had become hypersensitive to foreign terrorism, would have thought it legitimate to demand the head of any leader directly or indirectly involved in the painful attacks that left about 3,000 dead. But here again, nothing could be further from the truth. The CIA had quickly ruled out this theory, the information it had collected suggesting that Osama bin Laden's organization had never received assistance from the Iraqi state apparatus in the planning or the execution of the terrorist attacks. The idea that Saddam Hussein may have been linked to Al-Qaeda stemmed from erroneous information that made its way to Washington and the international press offices. This information related to the leader of the 9/11 hijackers, Mohamed Atta, and to an obscure member of the Iraqi secret service he supposedly met in Prague, Czech Republic. The table was then set, and all that was missing was the buffet, which some media were quick to provide. *The Associated Press* network, on September 18, 2001, published an article about the so-called Prague meeting between Mohammed Atta and not a member of the Iraqi secret service but a diplomat named Ahmed Khalil Ibrahim Samir Ani. A British newspaper, *The Observer*, went further on October 14, 2001, reporting that

Al-Qaeda militants had told the Egyptian authorities that their organization had obtained anthrax vials from the Iraqi government. Two weeks later, the *London Times* went on to reveal that Mohammed Atta had indeed taken possession of anthrax vials and that he had met with Iraqi officials on several occasions in various European cities. But the CIA had done its homework: data on Mohamed Atta's credit cards and phone calls, the agency said, showed that the Al-Qaeda hijacker was in Virginia at the time of the events attributed to him.

So, if the confiscation of the Iraqi oil industry, the theory on weapons of mass destruction and the trail of Al-Qaeda were not good reasons for the United States to intervene in Iraq, then why did that war happen? The answer lies in another theory that has been cast aside for too long by the media and experts of all kinds.

The New Century Must Belong to the Americans

In a 2007 interview with Amy Goodman of Democracy Now!, the retired general and former Supreme Allied Commander of NATO in Europe, Wesley Clark, revealed that a colleague of his, a general of the U.S. Joint Chiefs of Staff, had confessed to him that in the aftermath of 9/11, the Bush administration was planning to attack seven countries, namely Iraq, obviously, but also Syria, Lebanon, Libya, Somalia, Sudan, and Iran, over five years. Although it never materialized, this project was highly ambitious, but it was only an extension of an idea that had germinated a few years earlier in the minds of the hawks of the Republican Party.

* * *

Those hawkish minds had been toying with the idea of reshaping the Middle East, starting with Iraq. The plan had been detailed in a report that had gone unnoticed at that time, hidden behind the branches of the Lewinsky affair. This plan was the *Project for the New American Century* (PNAC). Based in Washington, DC, therefore in the back rooms of the White House, the PNAC's team was set up in 1997 by two prominent militarists, William Kristol and Robert Kagan. Both men's intentions were crystal clear: to promote U.S. leadership abroad. For, after all, a dominant America could only be beneficial to the world, according to these two intellectuals. And how should America exert its leadership? By "military force", why not. Kristol and Kagan were escorted by big names from the Republican clique: of the 25 personalities who signed the PNAC's founding statement of principles, ten served a few years later in the Bush administration, including Dick Cheney, Donald Rumsfeld, and Paul Wolfowitz.

The first signs of the PNAC appeared in a 1996 article published in *Foreign Affairs* magazine. The article, titled *Toward a Neo-Reaganite Foreign Policy*, suggested that the United States should resort to a foreign policy based on a kind of "benevolent global hegemony." A year later, the PNAC used barely more subtle formulas: for the coming century to be American, the government, it recommended, first needed to increase the defense budget, the nerve center of Uncle Sam's power, but it also had to make a top priority the advancement of political and economic freedoms overseas, which meant, "challeng[ing] regimes hostile to our interests and values." And the first of those hostile regimes targeted by Kristol and Kagan was, no surprise, Saddam Hussein's Iraq. In an open letter to President Bill Clinton, seven Republican personalities called for the overthrow of Saddam Hussein. These personalities were Donald Rumsfeld, Paul Wolfowitz, R. James Woolsey—who linked Iraq to the 9/11 attacks only two days after the events—, Elliot Abrams, Richard Perle, Robert Zoellick, and John Bolton. Clinton never followed up on the PNAC's initiative, probably because his vision of America was not focused on the need to show off its military superiority. Never mind, the hawks would get their revenge. In September 2000, just two months before the presidential elections, the PNAC published a report called *Rebuilding America's Defenses: Strategy, Forces, and Resources for a New Century*, one sentence of which would go down in history: "Further, the process of transformation, even if it brings revolutionary change, is likely to be a long one, absent some catastrophic and catalyzing event—like a new Pearl Harbor." Those who participated in the writing of that report were unaware that this "new Pearl Harbor" would arise one year later, on September 11, 2001.

When George W. Bush took on the presidency, all the stars were aligned for the PNAC, which then boasted several of the most influential members of the White House, to be given greater importance. Especially in the aftermath of 9/11, which paved the way for interventions in regions of the world suspected of harboring terrorists. At a meeting on September 14, where the President had convened his senior advisers, Paul Wolfowitz, Donald Rumsfeld's deputy in the Defense Department, explained that Al-Qaeda and the Taliban were only a part of the problem. Hamas and Hezbollah had to be taken into account as well, but there was another huge obstacle to be rid of, and this obstacle was, you guess it, Iraq. An alumnus of Princeton University, Wolfowitz was, in a way, the gray eminence of the Defense Department. But hidden behind the mask of this gray eminence was an authentic utopian, perhaps too much influenced by academic discourses. Donald Rumsfeld's deputy took pleasure in building a world steeped in American messianism, as if all American interventions had led to the establishment of democratic and egalitarian societies. One thing is sure, Wolfowitz was a great source of inspiration for President Bush. So much so that on September 17, the leader of the White House finally gave in: Iraq, he said to his advisers, was on his radar, but first, it was necessary to take care of Afghanistan. A few months later, in early 2002, the President signed a secret order authorizing the CIA to do everything to overthrow Saddam Hussein. The hawks could savor their victory.

Saddam Hussein, the West's Bastard

From then on, President Bush began to relay his interventionist propaganda, bringing up on a daily basis the idea that the world would be relieved if Iraqi dictator Saddam Hussein was removed from power. Thus, the conditions were met for the President to go on the offensive. His first step: trying to convince the American public of the need to intervene in Iraq while the dust of the 9/11 events had in part settled. If this persuasion campaign proved to be successful, the doors would be wide open to allow Washington to send troops to Iraq. Should only a minority of allied countries agree with the U.S. position did not matter to Bush and co.: Iraq was on the agenda, which meant that the United States was soon to start another war. The older Republicans, who had been waiting for a whole decade to finish off the work started during *Operation Desert Storm* in 1991, saw an opportunity for Bush II to avenge Bush I: the former was willing to launch a full-scale attack on Baghdad, something the latter had not done. The media, whose state of mind was weakened due to its indulgent attitude toward the Bush administration at a moment when 9/11 was still fresh in the collective memory, did not dare to question the President about the political past of his father, who was partly responsible for the rise of Saddam Hussein. Unknown to many, in the 80s, when George Herbert Walker Bush was walking down the corridors of the White House, first as Vice President then as President, the Iraqi government built up a massive military arsenal that aroused the envy of the Arab world thanks to America and its allies. Let's address this feature of history to better understand the phenomenon.

* * *

To begin with, we must look back in time, more precisely in 1979, a year of major upheavals in the Middle East. It was the year when the Shah of Iran was overthrown by religious fanatics in a revolution that led to the creation of an Islamist state headed by Ayatollah Ruhollah Khomeini. On the other side of the border, Saddam Hussein had just seized power and took a dim view of the Iranian maximalists who could at any time undermine his regime, especially since the new Iraqi President was at the helm of a country with a population mostly made up of Shiites, as in the neighboring republic. On September 22, 1980, under the guise of border disagreements, Iraq showered Iran with bombs, kicking off a war that was to end only eight years later. It was a war between two dictatorships, two middle powers that could make everything fall apart at any moment. But in Washington, the administration in place was convinced that it was the new Persian government, not its Sunni enemy, that mainly posed a threat to the U.S. interests in the Middle East. The hostage crisis would actually prove it right. Granted, Ayatollah Khomeini had spent time in France during his exile, but that experience did not have any impact on his approach toward the Western nations, against which he always felt a bitter hatred. At the White House, the goal was then clearly stated: Iraq had to defeat Iran. A goal that Ronald Reagan prioritized as soon as he became president in 1981, to the extent that the United States checked Iraq off its list of sponsors of terrorism, which enabled Saddam Hussein to qualify for financial loans from the American government. That was the reason why, in December 1983, Secretary of State George Shultz dispatched a special envoy to Baghdad, officially to discuss the war but unofficially to discuss business. This special envoy was Donald Rumsfeld, who would become Secretary of Defense under Bush II. This is a strange anecdote when you consider that the U.S. general staff knew that Saddam possessed chemical weapons he had already used against the Kurdish and Iranian populations. Officials in Washington were regularly tipped off about gas attacks carried out by the Iraqi Army and the CIA was aware of the location of every factory where Baghdad was producing its chemical weapons. Through thick and thin, the same Rumsfeld returned to Iraq the following year, notwithstanding that the United States had previously condemned the chemical weapons attacks, perhaps for the sake of improving its branding on the international stage. Whatever the meeting was about, Saddam Hussein, in his war against Iran, was able to benefit from the unquestionable support of the United States. Support firmed up by President Reagan as soon as he took office when he approved the sale of 60 Hugues and 10 Bell-Textron helicopters for, apparently, "civilian use." This is where lie the origins of the "Iraqgate."

The U.S. aid to the Iraqi state will ultimately extend until the invasion of Kuwait by Hussein's troops in 1990. In the 1985 to 1990 period alone, the United States guaranteed loans to Iraq worth $5.5 billion as part of the Department of Agriculture Business Credit Program. Those funds were obviously diverted for military purposes, but as early as 1987, Baghdad's finances deteriorated significantly. The Export-Import

Bank, a U.S. government agency responsible for allocating export credits, had to cover Iraq's defaults by granting more than $200 million a year as collateral. These defaults were caused by a debt that went up to $70 billion. In the first few months after the initial credits were granted, Iraq was already running out of money, $35 million to be exact. This was not a considerable amount, but even then, the Export-Import Bank responded by putting its aid on hold, a move that provoked a negative reaction at the White House, especially from Vice President George Bush who was quick to ask the Ex-Im leaders to reconsider their decision. In Washington, the only thing that counted was to restore the flow of credit in Iraq, which is why George Bush had to step in once again to ensure that the Export-Import Bank guarantees extra loans to Iraq worth $500 million for the construction of a pipeline. Always eager to bail out his ally in the Middle East, the future president approved a new billion-dollar loan in November 1989 to an Iraqi regime that was on the brink of collapse. Seven months later, he declared war on that same regime.

But before the war began, the smooth running of business between Baghdad and Washington had to be safeguarded, and this was done by leading personalities who played the role of intermediaries, even lobbyists. On the front line was Lawrence Eagleburger, Undersecretary of State for Political Affairs from 1982 to 1984, later president of the consulting firm Kissinger Associates, co-founded by Richard Nixon's ex-right-hand man, Henry Kissinger. Another key figure in the Iraqgate was Brent Scowcroft, vice president of Kissinger Associates before being appointed U.S. National Security Advisor. Despite his political functions, Scowcroft owned shares in forty companies that "coincidentally" obtained numerous export licenses for Iraq. These companies were, among others, General Motors, Volvo, Lockheed, General Electric, and ITT. Kissinger Associates, curiously cleared of all wrongdoing during the Iraqgate investigations, was close to the political power at the time, as much as it was an integral part of the U.S.-Iraq circle. Alan Stoga, its managing director, had ties with A. Robert Abboud, chairman of First City Bancorp of Texas, also a major lender to Iraq. But in parallel, Abboud was president of the United States-Iraq Business Forum, an organization that helped establish business partnerships between the United States and Iraq. Abboud, for a certain period, was also sitting on the board of directors of the First National Bank of Chicago, which had lent funds to Harken Energy, a company George W. Bush worked for as a consultant. Good relations are always useful in that field. Another example: the very boss of Kissinger Associates, Henry Kissinger, was, during that period, a paid member of the Consulting Board for International Policy of the Banca Nazionale del Lavoro (BNL), an Italian bank that provided hundreds of millions of dollars in loans to Saddam Hussein.

It is an understatement to say that a fair number of American companies found the Iraqi market quite appealing. The official (and incomplete) lists refer to about 91 companies that allegedly dealt with Saddam Hussein's government, most of the time via the Banca Nazionale del Lavoro. In the first quarter of 1989 alone, the Italian bank granted loans worth $565 million, all of which were earmarked for Iraqi military contracts. One of the companies that did business with Saddam Hussein, GM Heavy Truck Corp., worked on a project to build 5,000 heavy-duty vehicles for export to Iraq, partly financed by the BNL. Another one, Mack Truck, sold more than $9 million worth of trucks and military equipment through the BNL. In the same type of industry, Caterpillar entered into a $10 million market with Iraq, a sale once again financed by the Italian bank. The engineering firm Bechtel, on its side, was present in Iraq from 1988 until the invasion of Kuwait as a consultant on a petrochemical complex. Bechtel had signed a contract with Technical Corporation for Special Projects, a front company linked to the Iraqi military industry; the contract was worth an estimated $700 million. There are many other examples of this kind. In partnership with Matrix, a company that belonged to the Iraqi government, XYZ Options built a plant at the Al-Atheer nuclear complex, which was partly financed by the BNL for $14 million. XYZ also obtained letters of credit from the BNL for the sale of various supplies to the Iraqi State company Machinery Trading. Semetex, also thanks to the BNL, was involved in a $5 million project for the production of transistors, silicon diodes, and photovoltaic devices. Those materials were manufactured in a factory that supplied the Scuds missile launch sites. Servaas Inc. exported equipment for the construction of ammunition and artillery factories to Iraq as a result of a $40.6 million loan from the BNL contracted by the Iraqi government. Lincoln Electric also obtained a letter of credit from the BNL for the supply of machinery for the Iraqi military-industrial complex. The company sold, among other things, welding equipment used in Saddam Hussein's ballistic (Condor II) and nuclear programs. Similarly, Rotec Industries Inc. provided Iraq with conveyors valued at nearly $19 million, again thanks to the BNL. Sperry Corp., a former computer hardware and electronic equipment company, received a $1.3 million loan via the BNL, even though, as in the case of other companies mentioned above, the equipment was used for the production of ballistic missiles. As the scandal erupted following revelations about the role of the Banca Nazionale del Lavoro in the granting of loans to Iraq, the U.S. Agriculture Department owed the bank more than $350 million as a consequence of the near-bankruptcy of the Iraqi government. The Department, however, never suspended the loans that kept flooding Iraq until Hussein's troops invaded Kuwait. As proof: on August 1, 1990, just hours before Iraqi tanks crossed the Kuwaiti border, Washington approved the sale of $695,000 worth of data transmission devices to Baghdad.

Despite the collapse of his country's finances, Saddam Hussein had managed to build an impressive military arsenal, but equally impressive was its chemical and bacteriological weapons stockpile, thanks in large part to the good care of its Western allies. Among these allies was, of course, the United States, which, as it had done for the Iraqi military equipment, was quick to jump on the occasion to get access to this lucrative market. Plague, Clostridium botulinum, anthrax, salmonella, West Nile virus, Histoplasma capsulatam, Brucella melitensis, Clostridium perfringens, Clostridium tetani, products as obscure as their names landed in the Iraqi stocks without anyone asking for guarantees from those who had to handle them. In all, Washington approved the granting of 771 licenses for the export to Iraq of bacteriological agents and high-tech equipment for military purposes, for a global value of $1.5 billion. From 1985 to 1989, the American Type Culture Collection

(ATCC), a non-profit organization that collects, stores and distributes standard reference microorganisms, cell lines, and other materials for research and development, delivered 70 shipments of bacteria to Iraq, all of which had been approved by the U.S. Department of Commerce. On their part, Alcolac International, Nu Kraft Mercantile Corp., KBS and Phillips Export (now ConocoPhillips) supplied thiodiglycol, which is used in the manufacturing of mustard gas. Another company, Al-Haddad Enterprises, went so far as to sell 60 tons of DMMP, a material needed for the production of sarin gas, a deadly product. Baghdad even admitted to buying batches of anthrax from the Pasteur Institute in Paris. The spokesmen of the famous French institution had found nothing more to say than the Iraqi government had reassured them about the use of these products.

Germany was also among the main exporting countries to Iraq for products used in the manufacturing of chemical and bacteriological weapons. Nearly one hundred German companies conducted business with the Iraqi government. Preussag, imitating Al-Haddad Enterprises, exported products used to produce sarin gas, while Karl Kolb provided electronic equipment to test the effects of those toxic gases. But the Germans moved well beyond the chemical and bacteriological sectors, as they also tapped into the nuclear market. Engineers from NVA, an East German company, built a complex near Baghdad that the Iraqi Army used for nuclear program experiments. Another company, H & H Metalform G.m.b.H., had attempted to ship equipment to the Iraqi capital as part of the same program, but the shipment was seized at the Frankfurt Airport ten days after Saddam Hussein's troops invaded Kuwait. As per the export documents, H & H Metalform's gear was to be sent to a dairy plant, but it actually contained high-quality steel components. German authorities eventually discovered that the company was one of several suppliers to the Iraqi state of machinery meant for the production of nuclear weapons.

Reference was made earlier to a well-known French institution, the Institut Pasteur, but it was not the only one on that side of Europe involved in business dealings with Saddam Hussein's Iraq. France, like the United States and Germany, had well understood the full potential of the Iraqi market for its export products, a market from which its companies greatly profited. That is certainly the main reason why the French government opposed the 2003 American intervention in Iraq. At that time, the Iraqi state owed French companies no less than $4 billion for arms deals and infrastructure projects. The French business lobby, out of fear of having no chance to recover its money, urged the Chirac government to implore the United States to favor talks rather than confrontation. It is reported that the sole Thomson-CSF's order book for Iraq was worth $700 million, even though the Iraqi government owed this company $200 million. Thomson-CSF's mission was to assist Baghdad in setting up a factory for the production of military radars, radios, electronic jamming equipment and a device capable of triggering nuclear weapons. In all, French companies sold $5 billion worth of armored vehicles, missiles, combat aircraft and other military equipment to the Iraqi regime during Iraqgate. In addition to Thomson-CSF, Dassault Aviation, manufacturer of the renowned Mirage jet aircraft, also gained from the Iraqi windfall. And in association with China, France supplied Iraq with chemicals used in the manufacturing of fuel for long-range missiles. The French, it must be said, had a long history of political and commercial relations with the Iraqi state. Relations so close that during the second Gulf War, the Hexagon had the nerve to offer its support to the Iraqis so that they could escape the clutches of the Americans before the first cannon shots in March 2003. This is what the U.S. Army's intelligence services discovered when they seized a pile of French passports in the premises of the Iraqi government. This "betrayal" reminds us of the time when, during the Falklands War, France had sold Exocet missiles to the Argentine government, at war with the British. Talking about the British, they too wanted their piece of the pie in Iraq. Among other things to their credit: the construction of a chemical factory called Fallujah 2, out of which the government of Margaret Thatcher was fully aware of the use Iraq wanted to make. As one might say: Capital too often prevails over virtue. Seventeen British companies were suspected of dealing with the Iraqi state. Racal, a firm that contributed financially to Lady Thatcher's Conservative Party, was one of them. After signing a contract with Iraq in 1985, Racal obtained a secret defense grant of $42 million from the Export Credits Guarantee Department, the British equivalent of the U.S. Export-Import Bank. At the outbreak of the first Gulf War, the company was in the midst of building a factory on Iraqi soil.

What should we remember most from this period of British history? That the Thatcher government was not keen on investigating the negotiations surrounding the sale of weapons to Iraq. It was clear that the First Lady wished to keep her son Mark, who was deeply involved in the Iraqi quagmire, away from a possible lawsuit. In this circus, Mark Thatcher was linked to Carlos Cardoen, originally from Chile, whose company, Industrias Cardoen, was manufacturing cluster bombs. From 1984 to 1988, Industrias Cardoen sold more than $200 million worth of these cluster bombs to Iraq. The funds used by the Iraqi government to buy them passed through Geneva, Switzerland, then landed in bank accounts in Miami, Florida. There, a firm owned by the Chilean businessman, called Swissco Management Group, invested those funds in the real estate sector. This Cardoen was a tough cookie who did not like the idea of journalists sticking their noses in his business. In early 1990, Industrias Cardoen was about to sign a new contract with Baghdad when a British journalist, Jonathan Moyle, began investigating into its affairs. In the afternoon of March 1, 1990, Moyle's naked body was discovered in a closet by a maid working for a hotel in Santiago, Chile. The Chilean police initially believed that the journalist had committed suicide, but an autopsy quickly contradicted the results of the investigation. It was later learned that Cardoen, backed by the Iraqi government, was behind the murder. For the production of cluster bombs, Cardoen's main suppliers were Teledyne Industries, through its division Teledyne Wah Chang Albany, and International Signal and Control Corp. Swissco Management Group was found guilty of exporting 130 tons of zirconium—a metal used in the manufacturing of the cluster bombs—despite receiving the green light from the U.S. State Department to export to Iraq. A paradox that no one has tried to clarify yet. The company was fined $1.3 million and was denied the right to export for ten years. For Saddam Hussein's Iraq, Cardoen produced a total of 24,000 cluster bombs. So much for the Iraqgate.

Before the War, the Propaganda

Wars are never popular in Western nations. Governments always have to justify their decision to take part in an armed conflict by launching vast propaganda campaigns designed to convince their population of the legitimacy of the use of force. After 9/11, Americans were far from being won over by the prospect of intervening in Iraq as they did not see it as an absolute necessity, but that was before Washington and its media "allies" embarked on a large-scale operation aimed at "reprogramming" their mind. Among these media allies was a major newspaper: *The New York Times* (*NYT*), which, despite its historical antipathy toward the Republicans, quickly promoted the project put forward by the Bush administration and its militaristic rhetoric. Within hours of the intervention, one of the *NYT* columnists, Judith Miller, had promised her readers some great revelations about stocks of weapons of mass destruction (WMD) that Saddam Hussein had supposedly amassed. And she guaranteed that the skeptics would be confounded. "The Pentagon has deployed several new tactical units called mobile exploitation teams […] with state-of-the-art equipment and novel tactics to locate and survey at least 130 and as many as 1,400 possible weapons sites", the journalist wrote on March 19, 2003—the day of the intervention—, without ever being challenged by rational minds. We are still awaiting the discovery of only one of those sites. This Judith Miller ought to count herself lucky to have enjoyed the confidence of the *NYT*'s press room as she alone accounted for half of the fake news relayed by the U.S. media on Saddam Hussein's so-called weapons of mass destruction. And this was only the repetition of an act she performed in 1986 when she had fueled controversy in a series of articles she had written on Libya as part of a disinformation crusade against Muammar Gaddafi. Among other public figures who had orchestrated that crusade against Libya was Admiral John Poindexter, one of the Reagan Administration's top brass implicated at full steam in the Iran-Contra scandal. Nearly two decades later, in September 2002, Miller, this time, lashed out at Iraq, "revealing" that U.S. authorities had intercepted metal tubes meant for the Iraqi state's nuclear program, a statement contradicted in a report published by the Oak Ridge National Laboratory in Houston. But this did not matter to three secretaries, Condoleezza Rice, Colin Powell and Donald Rumsfeld, who relied on Miller's articles to state in front of the cameras that those tubes were evidence of the presence of WMDs in Iraq. The journalist later revived the debate by publishing another article in which she certified that weapons of mass destruction had indeed been found in Iraq; to say the contrary amounted to siding with the enemy. But on May 26, 2004, a week after the United States government cut ties with an Iraqi dissident called Ahmed Chalabi, the man behind the fake news campaign on the WMD, the *NYT*, through an editorial, made an open confession: part of Miller's articles on the Iraq dossier was strongly based on accounts of exiles opposed to the Iraqi regime, among them the infamous Ahmed Chalabi. In other words, the whole thing was a bunch of conspiracy theories and unconfirmed gossip. In the same breath, the newspaper said it regretted that "the controversial information [had] never been double-checked." This was a eureka moment for the *NYT* managers, but those have never admitted that they indirectly contributed to the deaths of tens of thousands of Iraqis and American soldiers.

The School of Media and Public Affairs, which sifted through 600 hours of the Iraqi war coverage on *CNN*, *ABC* and *Fox News* from the first American strikes to the fall of Baghdad, highlighted a rather worrying phenomenon: the majority of the reports written or broadcast by the major networks during this period were deeply sanitized. Only 13.5% of the reports, according to this school affiliated with the George Washington University, showed civilians or coalition soldiers killed during the battles. Another study, the Columbia University Project for Excellence in Journalism (which has since become the Journalism project of the Pew Research Center) roughly came to the same conclusions. It was not until much later that it was known why the media had become Washington's partners in crime. On April 20, 2008, *The New York Times*, which, by that time, seemed to be back on earth, revealed that it had gained access to 8,000 pages of documents, messages and recording notes that exposed a vast operation devised by the Defense Department jointly with the American media whose sole purpose was to promote the war in Iraq. At the center of this public relations campaign were former executives and senior officers of the United States military, portrayed as "military analysts" or "experts" for the circumstances. Those "analysts" and "experts" formed the fifth column of the Bush administration's pro-war propaganda. Dozens of faces thus became familiar to the viewers of the major news feeds, faces that belonged to men and women whose task was to relay the White House's warmongering rhetoric. But not only in the months leading up to the intervention in Iraq: ten of those "analysts" and "experts" were sent out to Guantanamo in 2005 to attest to the "quality of the facilities." Their observation: the prisoners were living in "very good conditions."

What the U.S. mainstream media had failed to mention was that most of the so-called "military analysts" had direct ties to the defense industry. Some were even lobbyists or members of boards of directors of companies that had everything to gain from a long conflict in Iraq. One of these "lobbyists", John Garrett, a former Marine colonel, had been recruited by *Fox News* while he was at the same time acting as a political adviser for Patton Boggs, a firm that helps businesses secure contracts with government agencies, including the Pentagon. Another one, Robert Scales Jr., also worked for *Fox News* while owning a military consulting firm. Two other *Fox* "analysts" were part of the defense sector: Lieutenant Colonel William Cowan and Major Robert Bevelacqua were chief executive officers and vice-presidents of WVC3 Group, a consulting firm that serves as a liaison between companies and the U.S. government. Two more examples: Lieutenant General Barry McCaffrey and retired Colonel Wayne Downing, both hired by the *NBC* network. Downing and McCaffrey were at the same time members of the Committee for the Liberation of Iraq, a lobby group formed with the avowed purpose of strengthening the public support for the U.S. intervention in Iraq. But McCaffrey had another hidden card: he was on the board of four defense companies—Mitretek, Veritas Capital, Raytheon Aerospace, and Integrated Defense Technologies—that hit the jackpot in Iraq.

All these "lobbyists" were directly connected to the White House and the Pentagon: private briefings with officials, tours in Iraq, access to classified documents, no privilege was lacking, as long as everyone closed ranks. At least one of those famous experts, Lieutenant Colonel Timur J. Eads, was honest enough to admit that he and his colleagues refrained from criticizing the Bush administration for fear that some "four-star" generals demand accountability.

Propaganda is not, however, the only tool used by governments to indoctrinate slavish minds. To the ideas, facts, or allegations spread deliberately to further a cause or damage an opposing one is added censorship, an essential element of any strategy whose goal is to prevent the propaganda from coming into conflict with contradicting messages. The U.S. military obviously used censorship on many occasions, for example in the summer of 2005 when the Pentagon refused to authorize the publication of an unclassified report from the RAND Corporation, a think tank funded by the federal government. The report was very critical of the White House, the Defense Department and other government agencies for their handling of the Iraq dossier. The RAND had put its finger on problems that, in its view, had deepened the crisis. The think thank blamed President Bush and his National Security Adviser, Condoleezza Rice, for failing to resolve disputes between rival organizations, particularly between Colin Powell's State Department and Donald Rumsfeld's Defense Department. The Rand, for that matter, was very harsh toward the Defense Secretary, describing him as being ill-qualified to lead the post-war reconstruction. The think thank had also claimed that General Tommy Franks, chief supervisor of the U.S. military operation in Iraq, had no clear view of what the army needed to do to secure the country after the American intervention. Franks and Rumsfeld, in the eyes of the RAND, had worsened the already disastrous consequences of the intervention by refusing to send sufficient troops after the fall of Baghdad. Poor planning, lack of organization and dissent within the Bush administration thus contributed to strengthening the determination of the insurgents at a time when resentment against the "negative effects of the American security presence" had gone up a notch. Those were all the blames that the U.S. government had wanted to hide from the American public.

The censorship aims, above all, to stifle speech and block images, and during the American engagement in Iraq, it mainly targeted the media that had adopted a different stance from the one favored by Washington. Such was the case with the *Al Jazeera* network, which was anathematized by the Bush administration, eager to silence the "scandalmongers" of the Qatari media. With that in mind, one could then state that this war caused other victims: the American viewers and readers, who, in the end, could only count on embedded journalists forced to blindly follow American troops across the Iraqi territory. Those journalists behave like sheep guided by their shepherds. But the *Al Jazeera* reporters were not relying on the United States military to feed their news wire, and this fact alone posed a serious threat to the Bush administration, a threat that could thwart its effort to hide the truth. Unlike the American media that only showed their obsequious side, *Al Jazeera* and, to a certain extent, *Al Arabiya*, from Saudi Arabia, did not shy away from showing death scenes and images of buildings destroyed by the American forces in the streets of major Iraqi cities. As a result, Washington counterattacked on April 9, 2004, by demanding that *Al Jazeera* remove all of its reporters from Fallujah, but the network dismissed the idea out of hand. It paid a heavy price for this decision. The following day, American jet fighters bombed the offices of the Qatari media in Fallujah as well as the home where one of its reporters, Ahmed Mansour, had spent the night, killing its owner. The consequences were such that for a few days, the network's live broadcast went off the air. On April 15, Defense Secretary Donald Rumsfeld, as he did so often, lost his temper, accusing *Al Jazeera* of broadcasting "vicious, inaccurate and inexcusable" reports. Ironically, twenty-four hours after Rumsfeld's scolding, *The Daily Mirror* revealed that President Bush had expressed to British Prime Minister Tony Blair his wish to shell Al Jazeera's offices in Qatar.

"The Largest Single Disaster in American Foreign Policy"

The *Shock and Awe* operation in Iraq turned out to be devastating for the country and its population, all the more so as the whole region is still suffering the consequences today. During the early days of the intervention, large cities like Baghdad, already plagued by the deluge of bombs and missiles dropped by the U.S. Air Force, were subjected to widespread looting. The average Iraqi, penniless and hungry, went after all institutions, public as private: government establishments, schools, universities, libraries, banks, businesses, hospitals and museums were "systematically stripped, emptied [and] ransacked." Even drilling rigs were said to be dismantled "for the hypothetical bits of copper" they contained. Those scenes were the daily lot of Iraq for at least ten weeks, at a time when American troops had lost control of the crowds. In this whole debacle, it is the black gold industry that suffered the most as Iraqi oil facilities were exposed to uninterrupted sabotage operations between May 2003 and September 2004. The whole thing ended up costing seven billion dollars to the state. One of the most important producers and exporters of oil, Iraq was then producing on average a little over 1,300,000 barrels per day at the height of the war, when it could easily produce a million more. The loss of earnings, in this regard, was estimated at $13 billion.

Since the Americans had turned Iraq upside down, they are the ones who inherited the task of leading the reconstruction program. Dispatched on the spot to act as governor, Paul Bremer, the strongman of the Coalition Provisional Authority (CPA), made a decision that marked a turning point in the Iraqi conflict and, above all, proved to be the triggering event of a movement that spread throughout Libya and Syria. Bremer believed that Iraq could not recover from the crisis as long as Saddam Hussein's men remained in power. He thus decided to dismantle the Baath Party, which had been holding the reins of the state since 1968. He did so through his infamous "Order 1", his very first decision on Iraqi soil. The mere fact of belonging to the Baath Party resulted in a dismissal for all its members. The "Order 2", the disbanding of the Iraqi Army, was just as harmful. These two decisions alone brought about the layoff of around 350,000 Iraqis—most of whom were men—who found themselves unemployed because of this arrogant America; an America that would soon discover that it had made 350,000 new enemies. Soldiers, doctors, lawyers and white collars, who had built up years of experience, lost their jobs in a critical time for the Iraqi reconstruction. Among these: Haji Bakr, a nationalist who, until then, had never been seduced by fundamentalism, felt deeply wronged by the Americans. It was Haji Bakr, along with a select group of former members of the Iraqi intelligence, who appointed Abu Bakr al-Baghdadi as ISIS's supreme leader in 2010. Pursuing this inconsistent approach, the U.S. administration chose an exile, who had spent the previous twenty-four years out of Iraq, to head the country. Nouri al-Maliki, a Shiite whose state of mind was absorbed by a feeling of revenge toward the Sunnis of the Baath Party, thus became Prime Minister of Iraq. And as his first official act, he chose Shiite supporters to hold senior government posts; Shiite supporters in a country hitherto run by Sunnis, it was, strictly speaking, an explosive recipe.

Paul Bremer's decrees sparked off anger not only among Iraqis but also among Americans, even in the Republican camp. The former Speaker of the House of Representatives, Newt Gingrich, went so far as to call Bremer "the largest single disaster in American foreign policy in modern times." Gingrich was so furious that he said about Bremer that he should have been relieved of his duties "no later than" September 2003. But the henchmen of the Bush administration could not care less about the former gray eminence of the 1994 Republican revolution. On December 14, 2004, President Bush awarded Bremer the "Presidential Medal of Freedom", the highest civilian award in the United States, for "especially meritorious contributions to the security or national interests of the United States, to world peace, or to cultural or other significant public or private endeavors." Bremer was also presented with the Defense Department award for "Distinguished Public Service", while the Richard Nixon Presidential Library and Museum honored him with the "Victory of Freedom Award" for "demonstrating leadership and working toward peace and freedom." You read that right: for "demonstrating leadership and working toward peace and freedom." To date, Bremer has never made his *mea culpa*. On the contrary, he has maintained his position against all odds: putting 350,000 Iraqis out of work, according to him, was the best decision to make in the circumstances.

All this chaos caused by the American intervention encouraged a fervent admirer of Al-Qaeda to try his luck in Iraq, where he sought to sow the seeds of revolt. For a time, Abu Musab al-Zarqawi, the forerunner of Abu Bakr al-Baghdadi, replaced Osama bin Laden in the collective mind, as much for those who opposed Islamic extremism as for those who supported it. Al-Zarqawi was not an Iraqi but a Jordanian, originally from Zarqa, to be more accurate. As a youngster, he became known as a thug with a violent temper. Quickly drawn into the criminal world, he got into the pimping and prostitution business, which perfectly symbolized his traits of character. These criminal activities led him straight to prison, where his personality underwent a complete transformation. For the first time in his life, al-Zarqawi turned out to be a sort of leader for his community; but at the same time, this transformation guided him toward the jihad. In his dreams, he saw himself as the head of a large Islamic state, but before reaching this goal, he needed to make a transit journey to Kandahar, where those who aspired to take part in the fight for Allah were receiving training. Inebriated by the scent of the battlefield, al-Zarqawi then joined Al-Qaeda and the Taliban in their stronghold. Unfortunately for him, he hit a wall. Osama bin Laden and Ayman al-Zawahiri were not at all impressed by the Jordanian, whom they deemed too brutal for their liking, which spoke volumes about the man's character. Despite everything, the future jihadist leader left Kandahar with his head held high and the determination to show that the two Al-Qaeda's strongmen were just wrong about his personality. Paradoxically, it is the Americans who would offer him a golden opportunity to prove himself. In 2002, when George W. Bush was actively trying to convince his allies of the need to invade Iraq, the Jordanian moved up to a terrorist training camp in northern Iraq, on Iran's border. That relocation worried the CIA, which was monitoring the camp thanks to the few agents it had planted inside its walls. In Langley, everyone knew that jihadists were manufacturing chemical and bacteriological weapons in that camp, a reason that had incited the agency to seek Washington's support for a preemptive strike. But in the American capital, the administration was planning the overthrow of Saddam Hussein and al-Zarqawi was an invaluable asset in this daring project. Why is that? Because Dick Cheney had decided to use him just to prove that Al-Qaeda and the Iraqi regime were maintaining fraternal ties. Ties that the CIA has never been able to demonstrate, which did not prevent Cheney and his cohort from claiming otherwise.

It was to the same CIA, more precisely to the Directorate of Analysis, that Secretary of State Colin Powell had assigned the task of proofreading and editing the historical speech he was to deliver to the United Nations Security Council with the aim of persuading the allies that Saddam Hussein posed an immediate danger to global security. Powell had full confidence in the intelligence agency, a confidence that was not shared by everyone within the Bush government, especially in Vice President Cheney's office, where the CIA's stance on Al-Qaeda and the Iraqi regime was viewed with skepticism and contempt. Skepticism and contempt that would rub off on the speech of the Secretary of State. When the latter addressed the panel of the Security Council to promote the military intervention in Iraq, those who had worked on the editing and proofreading of the speech noticed, as they were listening, that there was something wrong. Almost nothing of what had been added and edited in the speech came out of Powell's mouth. It was only later that the former Secretary of State learned that the office of the Vice Presidency had reedited and rewritten the main lines of the speech to make sure it served the interests of the administration. Powell has never explained why he had been so easily fooled by his Vice President. During his famous speech, the former Secretary of State named Abu Musab al-Zarqawi twenty-one times. The link between Al-Qaeda and Saddam Hussein was thus confirmed in front of the allies, which allowed the U.S. government to proceed to the next step: the military intervention. But Cheney and his stooges were not done with the CIA. The conservative circle had come to believe that Langley was closer to the Democrats than the Republicans. In the period following the overthrow of Saddam Hussein, then-CIA analyst Nada Bakos wrote a Presidential Daily Brief (PDB) in which she pointed out that Abu Musab al-Zarqawi's network was behind the main insurgent attacks. The PDB stood out for its transparency: "I wrote a Presidential Daily Brief based on intelligence that we had received, that Zarqawi was responsible for some of the major initial attacks in 2003, that he was still there, and that he was looking to foment civil war", said Bakos in a *PBS* documentary. In the Vice President's office, the memo's conclusion was thought to be a little too apocalyptic. If made public, that PDB would likely contribute to a drastic shift in public opinion, Cheney and his staff believed. Consequently, something had to be done. It was then that Nada Bakos received a call from Lewis "Scooter" Libby, Dick Cheney's Chief of Staff, who wanted to convince her that there was no such thing as an insurgency in Iraq, let alone a civil war. At that moment, the former intelligence analyst "felt like I was being questioned about my analysis." Within the CIA, everyone seemed to have forgotten that all that mattered for Washington was promoting the war, not avoiding it. And in Iraq, everything was going through Abu Musab al-Zarqawi. His sudden and violent attacks captivated the Islamic world but annoyed Al-Qaeda leaders. In a letter he sent to al-Zarqawi, Ayman al-Zawahiri urged him to cease all action against Muslims. But the Jordanian terrorist disregarded those directives and even challenged al-Zawahiri by increasing the war effort against the Iraqi Shiites. Explosions, mass killings, beheadings, Al-Qaeda in Iraq completely reinvented terrorism and became a source of inspiration for a whole generation of jihadists who would storm the barricades in future conflicts, particularly in Syria. It was al-Zarqawi who first used the Internet as a propaganda tool. His *alter ego*, Abu Bakr al-Baghdadi, was at the time locked up in Iraqi prisons, where he would meet former officers of Saddam Hussein's army. Once released, al-Baghdadi rose through the ranks within Iraq's jihadist ring until he became the head of what would become the Islamic State.

Meanwhile, a U.S. intelligence report released on January 14, 2005, confirmed what any observer had already suspected. The report came from the National Intelligence Council, an organization whose main task is to devise future intelligence strategies. The report's conclusion was unequivocal: Iraq, it said, had replaced Afghanistan as a playground for the next linage of "professional" terrorists. Four months later, the CIA followed suit, arguing that Iraq might well be more important to jihadists than Afghanistan was during the best years of Al-Qaeda, noting that the country was then serving as a "laboratory" for urban guerrillas. The following year, a *National Intelligence Estimate* (NIE), an analysis report prepared by the sixteen intelligence agencies of the United States, spoke of Iraq as the "cause celebre" for jihadists. Another report, that one produced by the Center on Law and Security, concluded that "the Iraq occupation [was] directly to blame for an upsurge in fundamentalist violence worldwide." All these conclusions would be brushed aside by the hawks of the Bush administration.

Billions of Dollars Gone Missing

Just a few months after the start of the American intervention in Iraq, it was learned that $774,300 were reported missing from the coffers of the Coalition Provisional Authority (CPA), run by the "illustrious" Paul Bremer, the man to whom the Bush administration had handed over the bridles of the initial post-Saddam Hussein period, as we have previously seen. This sum was not especially large by American standards, yet, it portended a plague that would take the occupier into an endless spiral of fraudulent practices. A year after this revelation, *The Guardian* reported that an investigation had been opened into a fraud committed by officials from the south-central division of the Iraqi reconstruction committee in the city of Hillah. In a single year, about $100 million belonging to this committee had evaporated, as if by magic. At the heart of the investigation were U.S. military officers, civilian employees of the Defense Department and contractors from various sectors. According to *The Guardian*, the institutions and infrastructures that were to benefit from this money—schools, hospitals, aqueducts, power plants—were in ruins and therefore needed a quick injection of cash to be restored. Those are only a few examples of many cases of funds unaccounted for that had been uncovered by auditors.

The figures, as of January 30, 2005, were astronomical: $8.8 billion, this was the amount the U.S. administration had lost track of; $8.8 billion that was coming right from the reserves of the directorate responsible for the Iraqi reconstruction.

It was the International Advisory and Monitoring Board (IAMB), the audit oversight body for the Development Fund for Iraq, that had first blown the whistle about these irregularities. Those billions amounted to the entire Iraqi interim government spending from October 2003 through June 2004. But more surprises of this kind awaited the auditors, who turned their eyes, for a time, to a "flagship organization": Paul Bremer's Coalition Provisional Authority. The CPA had at its disposal a $16 billion fund derived from the economic activities of the Iraqi government: $6 billion came from what was left over from the UN Oil for Food Programme, and at least $10 billion were the result of resumed Iraqi oil exports. Still, Bremer's organization had drawn a total of $20 billion out of the funds belonging to the Iraqi government, which was $4 billion more than what had been set aside for it. Four billion dollars was coincidentally the sum written off the accounting books that registered Iraqi exports. Those data had been released by Christian Aid, the official relief and development agency of 41 Protestant and Orthodox churches in the UK and Ireland. Christian Aid had noted that of the $10 billion derived from the Iraqi exports, only $6 billion had been accounted for. The *BBC*, which had broadcast a report on the embezzlement in Iraq, had interviewed retired Admiral David Oliver, a former member of the finance oversight committee for the CPA. The English network wanted to get the admiral's opinion on the billions that had disappeared into thin air. Oliver's response was revealing of the arrogance demonstrated by the American delegation: "I can't tell you whether or not the money went to the right things or didn't—nor do I actually think it's important", the retired Admiral had said, dryly. That arrogance was felt in all spheres of activity during the American occupation. The International Advisory and Monitoring Board, cited above, had discovered that more than 100 contracts worth billions of dollars had been awarded without competitive bidding. A hospital administrator had told *The Guardian* that an officer representing the

CPA had crossed out the original price that appeared on a supply contract and doubled it because he wanted to offer himself an "extra" for his retirement allowance. That is how the CPA managed the funds for the reconstruction of Iraq. When members of the Iraqi Governing Council asked Paul Bremer why the contract to repair a cement factory in Samarah was going to cost $60 million instead of $20 million as originally planned, they were told that they should just thank the coalition for the ousting of Saddam Hussein. Iraqi businessmen repeatedly complained about the bribes they had to lay on the table only to obtain the right to answer a call for bids from the CPA. Millions were also billed for works that have never been done. An example: $3,379,505 for a repair contract over a pipeline, even though no employee went to the site to carry out the said repairs. It was common knowledge that thousands of "ghost employees" were paid for no reason. The auditors had investigated at least 69 such cases, most of which were related to theft, fraud, and extortion. One of those cases involved a payroll of 8,206 employees when barely 600 of them could be identified. As if that were not enough, on February 15, 2007, auditors from the Defense Contract Audit Agency (DCAA) informed the House Committee on Oversight and Government Reform, the main investigative committee of the United States House of Representatives, that "contractors in Iraq submitted about $5.1 billion in unsupported costs and $4.9 billion in questionable costs (for which contractors lack proper documentation)." Of that $10 billion, $2.7 billion was attributable to the Halliburton company alone, a former employer of then-Vice President Dick Cheney.

The first victims of these fraudulent practices were, of course, the Iraqis. Millions were "lost" at the Central Bank of Iraq, without anyone knowing how such a thing could have happened. Properties seized by the CPA, valued at between $11 million and $26 million, have never been accounted for. What did Bremer's organization do with these properties? Who knows. Another troubling fact: in the weeks leading up to Paul Bremer's leaving from Iraq, the CPA had hastily awarded multiple contracts worth $3 billion, drawn out of Iraqi funds. Luckily, auditors had been able to look into the accounting records of the U.S.

Embassy in Baghdad, to which the management of these contracts had been entrusted. Their report was rather striking: 225 contracts worth $327 million were unaccounted for. The auditors had also reviewed another series of contracts which they had been unable to prove that goods and services had been received for 154 of them. Bremer himself, it was found, had at one point a $600 million slush fund at his disposal. But the thing is that this slush fund had not appeared in any administrative document. And of these $600 million, $200 million were reportedly concealed in one of Saddam Hussein's former palaces, for reasons that only Paul Bremer knows. The story, unfortunately, does not end here. Stuart W. Bowen Jr., a friend of President Bush, discovered that between $1.2 billion and $1.6 billion in cash and $200 million in gold bullion had been stolen and transferred to a bunker in rural Lebanon for safekeeping. Bowen, who had been specifically appointed to investigate the financial chaos in Iraq, was never able to obtain the support of either the Bush administration or the Obama administration to help him get those assets back. The CIA, which was well equipped to investigate the matter, showed no interest in it, according to Bowen, while the FBI argued that it was outside its jurisdiction. Two of Bowen's team investigators have never been able to obtain permission to enter the bunker. This case has not resurfaced since then.

Millions of Weapons Lost in the Desert Sand

When you take into account the history of U.S. interventions around the world, you notice that the American government rarely learns from its mistakes. In Iraq, nobody seemed to have remembered that two decades earlier, more than a thousand Stinger surface-to-air missiles, which had been supplied by the United States to the mujahideen opposed to the Soviet Union in Afghanistan, had landed on the black market, therefore in the hands of jihadist groups such as Al-Qaeda. The CIA had to pay two, in some cases three or even four times, the original price to take those missiles back, whose initial cost could amount to several tens of thousands of dollars each. Fast forward to 2004. On November 7, *The Washington Post* reported that the Afghan scenario was back but this time in Iraq: nearly 6,000 portable missile systems drawn out of Saddam Hussein's stocks had gone off the radar. Too proud to show their military superiority against a poorly resourced army, the Americans never saw fit to secure the weapons depots of the former Iraqi regime. Hussein, over the years, had acquired 5,600 Russian-made SA-7 portable missiles. The problem is: it was too late when intelligence services learned that these missiles had likely been sold back to the rebels. These weapons, known as MANPADS, for Man-Portable Air-Defense Systems, can pose a danger to airliners. At low altitude, aircraft are an easy target. In 2002, a terrorist group launched two missiles from one of these devices, targeting an airplane that was about to take off at Mombasa airport in Kenya. In 2003, the U.S. State Department had estimated the number of aircraft hit by MANPADS at 40 since the 70s, which had led to 24 crashes and 600 deaths. Ironically, in November 2003, a Chinook CH-47 transport helicopter was struck head-on west of Baghdad by one of those MANPADS, killing 16 American soldiers and wounding 20. In 2015, ISIS also used an SA-7 against a U.S. aircraft backing up the Iraqi army and the Kurds. In Iraq, hundreds of MANPADS have reportedly been recovered, but the vast majority have gone missing.

Baghdad had built up a significant arsenal: missile launchers, as we have just seen, but also stacks of weapons and ammunition, which were dispersed in caches all over the country. Those caches were discovered in schools, mosques, hospitals, and warehouses, or in various places in the Euphrates and Tigris valley. In September 2003, General John Abizaid, the head of the U.S. Central Command, was forced to admit, before the Senate, that his troops had lost control of the resale of those weapons on the black market. Abizaid had evaluated the amount of unsecured ammunition to be 650,000 tons spread over thousands of sites. Also in 2003, the Defense Department was granted new authorities by the U.S. Congress to more flexibly and rapidly transfer arms to Iraq via the Iraq Relief and Reconstruction Fund, later renamed Iraq Security Forces Fund. With those privileges, the Defense Department no longer had to comply with the law and "unbearable" constraints such as human rights. Arms transfers, for that matter, were also excluded from the U.S. government's annual reports. So, as Saddam Hussein's former army's hardware was flourishing on the underground market, the American military was transferring at least one million small arms and millions of ammunition. Kalashnikovs, RPG-7s, assault rifles, Glock pistols and other war tools were delivered to the Iraqi forces not only from the United States, but also from other countries. In this regard, in 2007, the Iraqi government stroke a $100 million deal for the purchase of small arms from China. On September 25 of that year, the United States Defense Security Cooperation Agency announced the opening of a $2.2 billion market for the supply of weapons and military equipment to Iraq, which comprised 120,000 M-16A4 and 12,035 M-4 assault rifles. In 2008, Iraq bought 80,000 more M-16A4 rifles from the U.S. government and signed another contract, this time worth $236 million, with Serbia for the supply of a wide range of weapons and military equipment, including assault rifles (M-21 and older M-70 models), sub-machine guns, pistols, anti-tank rockets, mortar shells, ammunition, and explosives. As expected, too many of those transactions were handled "in a disorganized fashion", according to John Holly, a former director of reconstruction logistics for the U.S.-led Coalition Provisional Authority from 2003 to 2008. "There was no centralized database of what we had procured for the Iraqis", Holly said to the Centre for Public Integrity. This statement, though, was false, at least in part: the Americans did create databases; the problem is that they were barely used. In October 2006, a report by the Special Inspector General for Iraq Reconstruction (SIGIR) determined that only 2.7% of the 370,000 infantry weapons supplied to the Iraqi security forces "had details of the serial numbers [...] logged in the U.S. Department of Defense inventories", according to the Organized Crime and Corruption Reporting Project (OCCRP). In December 2007, a report by the Defense Department's Inspector General concluded that over $1 billion worth of weapons and military equipment shipped by the United States to the same Iraqi security forces could not be found or accounted for. In all, approximately 190,000 weapons had been "lost" for the period from June 2004 to December 2005 only. And here, "lost" can be considered a euphemism that strictly serves to hide the fact that the weapons had been stolen and resold on the black market. The case had caused a scandal in the United States and prompted the resignation of one of the Defense Department's officials, Claude Bolton, who was at the time Assistant Secretary of the Army for acquisition, logistics, and technology. An organization called Action on Armed Violence (AOAV) drew up an exhaustive list of the weapons the United States supplied to Iraq and Afghanistan from September 11, 2001, to September 10, 2015. A team of AOAV researchers spent almost a year investigating all contracts issued by the Pentagon during those 14 years and the results of the research were reported by *The New York Times* (*NYT*). According to the AOAV, assuming that the data may have been slightly underestimated, the Pentagon delivered nearly 1.5 million firearms to various Afghan and Iraqi security forces, including more than 978,000 assault rifles, 266,000 pistols and approximately 112,000 submachine guns. Now, according to the researchers, the Pentagon kept track of only 700,000 of those firearms, or 48% "of the total small arms supplied by the U.S. government that can be found in open-source government reports", as the *NYT* stated. Another report, this one published in 2007 by the United States Government Accountability Office, noted that 110,000 Kalashnikov assault rifles and 80,000 pistols transferred to the Iraqi security forces could not be accounted for. Again, history repeats itself, as a recent audit of the Defense Department pointed out that the "1ˢᵗ TSC [1ˢᵗ Theater Sustainment Command, a subordinate unit of the army responsible for operational and logistical support] could not provide complete data for the quantity and dollar value of equipment on hand" regarding the military hardware that was sent to Iraq and Kuwait to supply the Iraqi Army in its campaign against the Islamic State. The deliveries in question included tens of thousands of assault rifles, ammunition, and hundreds of Humvees. And according to *The Washington Post*, the Pentagon has lost track of $500 million worth of arms stocks in Yemen, a country at war against Saudi Arabia. U.S. officials fear that those arms could have been seized by Iranian-backed rebels or by Al-Qaeda. Among the weapons and military equipment missing are two Huey helicopters and 160 Humvees.

No Quarter for the Civilians

In Washington, officials want us to believe that war crimes are foreign to American culture. Yet, when one closely looks into this issue, one quickly realizes that this culture is not immune to blunders. As proof: the case of the infamous napalm, a product that was supposed to be buried forever in the history books of the Vietnam War. The Protocol III on the prohibition or limitation of the use of incendiary weapons is explicit: the use of napalm against civilian populations is strictly forbidden. Although the United States has always refused to join that convention, the U.S. Army nevertheless claimed to have destroyed its arsenal in 2001. It was a half-lie. In August 2003, a Marine Corps colonel, Mark Daly, was forced to admit that Mark 77 bombs, which some compare to napalm bombs, had been used by the U.S. Air Force in Iraq. The news had first been brought to the attention of the public by an Australian journalist who had reported that American jet fighters had dropped 500 Mark 77 over Safwan Hill, near the Kuwaiti border, on oil-filled trenches that the old Iraqi regime had dug. The United States also used these bombs in Afghanistan, in particular during the battle of Tora Bora in the fall of 2001. But there's more: white phosphorus-based bombs, also known as *Willy Pete* or *Whiskey Pete*, were used against the Iraqi city of Fallujah. In case you don't know, white phosphorus ammunition, upon explosion, spread particles over a wide area, which particles burn spontaneously in the air until they all disappear. The smoke easily penetrates clothing, even protective gear, and burns skin and flesh down to the bone. We can easily imagine the rest.

It is also in Fallujah, at around the same time it was learned that the U.S. Military had used incendiary bombs, that American soldiers killed 13 demonstrators who were protesting against the occupation of the Al-Qaed school. U.S. Army's spokesmen had then claimed that the soldiers, while taking up positions on the roof of the building, had been targeted by men armed with AK-47 assault rifles. But in a report published after the events, Human Rights Watch (HRW) had disputed these allegations, stating that no demonstrator had been in possession of a weapon. A correspondent for *The Independent*, Phil Reeves, echoed that conclusion, saying that no bullet holes were visible on the Al-Qaed school's facade in the minutes after the assault, which proved that no one in the crowd could have fired on the American soldiers. According to eyewitnesses, the battalion had even shot at those providing care for the wounded and blocked access to the rescue teams. Fallujah had already been marked by a massacre that had occurred on February 13, 1991, during the first Gulf War. A bombing mission to destroy a simple bridge had turned into a bloodbath: 130 civilians had died, and around 80 had been injured. Three Tornado missiles dropped by the British Air Force had missed their target and at least one of them had struck an apartment building. Perhaps the demonstrators had this carnage in mind when they showed up at the Al-Qaed school. This latter sad event, however, did not remain unanswered. Thousands of Fallujah citizens gathered the next day in front of the former headquarters of the Baath Party, occupied by the U.S. Army, to protest against these war crimes and demand the withdrawal of the American troops from the city. It was a predictable scenario that triggered an equally predictable reaction: four people were killed by snipers, and fifteen others were injured during the protests. Again, the American commanders pleaded self-defense, but a reporter had another opinion on the matter. As Human Rights Watch and Phil Reeves had done in the Al-Qaed school case, P. Mitchell Prothero, of the *United Press International* network, stated that no demonstrator carried a weapon that day. The only bullet casings found on the site came from the weapons used by the American troops. A few months before those deadly clashes, more precisely on April 7, 2004, a Bell AH-1W Cobra attack helicopter had launched a Hellfire missile on the Abdul-Aziz al-Samarrai mosque, once again in Fallujah, on the ground that insurgents had taken refuge in it. An F-16 fighter had followed by dropping a 500-pound bomb on the mosque, in clear violation of the Geneva Convention that prohibits attacks on religious buildings. According to witnesses, about 40 people were killed during this strike. In their defense, Marine Corps officials claimed that the mosque had lost its status as a protected place because it had housed insurgents, thus becoming a "legitimate military target." In all likelihood, the American forces had vowed to bring to heel the residents of

Fallujah who had the tendency to revolt. That is why the U.S. troops had laid siege to the city, shelling entire neighborhoods and power plants with bombs of 500, 1,000, and even 2,000 pounds. Fallujah was then plunged into darkness and quickly ran out of food. The few journalists authorized to enter the city described horror scenes in hospitals, schools, and mosques.

Fallujah experienced many traumatic episodes, in fact. Apart from those mentioned above, another one was kept in memory under the name of *Operation Phantom Fury*, carried out in November and December 2004 with the aim of retaking the city from the hands of the insurgents. Between 4,000 and 6,000 Iraqis were killed and 70% of the buildings destroyed throughout this offensive which lasted more than two weeks. Over 200,000 residents had to flee the city. The UN Special Rapporteur had accused the United States of "using hunger and deprivation of water as a weapon of war against the civilian population" during the siege. The U.S. troops had gone so far as to exclude the Red Cross, the Red Crescent, and even journalists from the area. All males between 15 and 55 years old had been forced to stay in the city. Burhan Fasa'am, a Lebanese photographer, said that snipers positioned on the roof of a hospital were "shooting on everyone", adding that "with no medical supplies, people died from their wounds." In fact, those who were brave enough to stroll down the streets of the city "[were] a target for the Americans." A citizen asserted that he had seen U.S. Army tanks rolling "over the wounded on the streets" several times. Another one recalled: "They shot women and old men in the streets. Then they shot anyone who tried to get their bodies." U.S. fighters had also dropped three bombs on a healthcare center, killing 35 patients and 15 workers. By the end of *Operation Phantom Fury*, which could easily be described as a crime against humanity, 36,000 to 50,000 Fallujah homes had been destroyed, along with 60 schools and 65 mosques. Hala Jaber, the last journalist to leave the city before the start of the military assault and the first to return there months later, wrote, more than a year after *Phantom Fury*, that "the actions of U.S. and Iraqi forces [had] reignited the insurgency. Anger, hate, and mistrust of America [were] deeper than ever." But war crimes were not only committed in Fallujah. On November 19, 2005, a group of Marines shot dead 24 civilians in Haditha, a town in the western province of Al-Anbar, Iraq. Men, but also women, children and elderly were shot multiple times at point-blank range, even though they were unarmed. A statement issued by the Marines first announced that 15 civilians and 8 insurgents had been killed by the explosion of a bomb in response to an attack on a military convoy. But due to pressure from the media, which became more critical of U.S. policies with time, the U.S. Military had resolved to tell the truth and open an investigation into this unprovoked attack.

God knows there were plenty of massacres in Iraq during the American intervention, but the following account is beyond what most people could ever imagine in their lives. On March 12, 2006, four soldiers from the 502nd Infantry Regiment raped a teenage girl, Abeer Qassim Hamza, before killing her and all members of her family. The event, which went down in history as the *Mahmoudiyah Massacre*, took place in the village of Yusufiyah. The four men went to the family home with the sole purpose of raping the girl. On the spot, one of the soldiers, Steven Dale Green, killed Abeer's parents and little sister, while two other soldiers raped the teenager. Green, in turn, raped Abeer, then shot her in the head. After committing their crime, the soldiers set fire to Abeer's lower body to remove all traces of rape. The fire eventually spread throughout the house and the smoke alerted neighbors who were among the first to discover the sinister scene. Fortunately, justice prevailed: Steven Dale Green was charged with raping and murdering; he received a life sentence but committed suicide behind bars in 2014. The other three received sentences of 90 to 110 years in prison.

In February 2006, the Prosecutor of the International Criminal Court (ICC) revealed that he had received 240 complaints related to the invasion of Iraq, therefore since March 2003, all of them concerning war crimes. But since the United States is not a member of the ICC, no lawsuits have been filed.

James Steele's Death Squads

Sooner or later, Iraq had to return to the Iraqis. The dismantling of the Baath Party and the Iraqi Army had left a gaping hole in the Iraqi society, particularly within the police force. In Washington, it was then decided to reintroduce an old tactic that had proven its worth in Central America during the 1980s: the formation of "death squads." Two technocrats were selected to lead those professional assassins' training programs: John Negroponte and Robert Stephen Ford. Ford would later become the U.S. ambassador to Syria in the first years of the conflict. For John Negroponte, the scene was familiar as he had taken up a front-row seat during the creation of Nicaragua's death squads throughout the Contras era. This former Reagan henchman was, at that time, the American Ambassador to Honduras, a prosperous period for that country as U.S. military aid had grown from $4 million to over $75 million a year thanks to the good care of Negroponte. President Reagan had thought it a good idea to replace Negroponte's predecessor, Jack Binns, first because he was Jimmy Carter's man, then because he was too talkative for his liking. Binns had repeatedly complained about human rights violations committed by the Honduran Army under the government of Policarpo Paz Garcia. Negroponte, who was his opposite, had clearly understood his role: remain silent on Honduras's state crimes, which was all the more necessary as Paz Garcia fully supported the United States in its war against the Sandinistas of Nicaragua. Twenty years later in Iraq, Negroponte, in addition to Robert Stephen Ford, was flanked by an old acquaintance from the days of the Contras: James Steele, a retired colonel whose official title was "advisor to the Iraqi security forces." Steele was the man on the ground, the one who would turn his organizations into true killing machines. Years before, the former colonel had himself shown his true colors in Nicaragua and El Salvador. Celerino Castillo, a former Drug Enforcement Administration (DEA) agent based in El Salvador in the 1980s, remembers him quite well: "I first heard about Colonel James Steele going to Iraq and I said they're going to implement what is known as the *Salvadoran Option* in Iraq and that's exactly what happened. And I was devastated because I knew the atrocities that were going to occur in Iraq which we knew had occurred in El Salvador", Castillo said to *The Guardian*. Steele's brutal methods had not gone unnoticed in 1989 by Dick Cheney himself who approached the colonel to set up a new police force in Panama, following the overthrow of Manuel Noriega, and to act as the principal link between the new Panamanian government and the U.S. military. Cheney had surely this period in mind when, along with Negroponte, he brought Steele back at work in Iraq.

James Steele was indeed the perfect man to train death troops in Iraq. And he did such a "good job" that his squads quickly dragged Iraq into a tsunami of uncontrollable violence. In this regard, the head of the United Nations delegation for human rights in Iraq, John Pace, had tried to grab Washington's attention to an overwhelming figure: hundreds of people, he had said, were tortured and murdered every month in Baghdad by the Iraqi Interior Ministry's death squads. In short, by the troops trained by Steele. One of these troops would become famous: the Wolf Brigade, whose members came from the lower layers of the Shiite community in Iraq. The Wolf Brigade had 2,000 members ready to fight with the Sunnis who had persecuted them during Saddam Hussein's reign. According to a confidential cable dated June 16, 2005, 25 cases related to the Wolf Brigade, involving abuses committed against Sunni prisoners, had until then been investigated. Those cases had resulted in at least one death, as reported by official figures, although testimonies on the field show a starkly different picture. One of the Wolf Brigade's victims, Muataz Salah Ahmed, told *The Guardian* that some of the organization's thugs had assaulted his wife after threatening to rape her. Four of his colleagues from the hotel where he worked were killed in front of him. The same thugs had drilled holes in his arms and legs. Locked up for eight months in a poorly maintained and overcrowded prison, he was released by a court without ever being charged. On May 8, 2007, more thugs from the same brigade, accompanied by U.S. soldiers, raided Baghdad's Al-Rashid neighborhood, arresting a dozen men. For obscure reasons, the Americans left those men in the hands of the Shiite gang. Consequently, eight of them were later found dead in a mosque; the other ones disappeared. The Wolf Brigade was also engaged in kidnappings and one of them involved the son of the head of a political coalition in Iraq. The brigade demanded a $500,000 ransom to Tawfiq al-Yasiri, of the Democratic Patriotic Coalition, whose family finally managed to raise $220,000 for his son's release. If we are to believe the former Iraqi general Muntadher al-Samari, in Baghdad only, a little more than a dozen secret prisons were under the control of the Interior Ministry and used by the special police commandos, therefore by James Steele's hoodlums. A U.S. soldier from the 69th Armor Regiment deployed to Samarra in 2005 stated: "It was like the […] Gestapo, basically. [The commandos] tortured anyone suspected […] of being part of the insurrection." The Wolf Brigade was finally disbanded and replaced by the Muthanna Brigade. Predictably, this new version employed the same procedures. The head of the Muthanna Brigade, Nassir al-Hiti, got rich thanks to the very lucrative kidnapping for ransom industry. Profits quickly accumulated in the pockets of the general and his chief officers as $15,000 were asked for each victim. As for the detainees, they were certainly not in a more enviable position in the presence of the Muthanna Brigade. Cases of torture, murders and arbitrary arrests grew rapidly during the rule of this other squad. The Volcano Brigade, another pure product of the Steele team, also haunted the streets of major Iraqi cities. Suffice to recall this massacre reported by the *BBC* on May 31, 2005, which took place in a Baghdad district where the brigade had sent shock troops, killing 76 people, not without first torturing them.

Like many others before and after him, James Steele has never had to face justice for the Iraqi bloodbath. For a moment, *The Guardian* sought to interview him so he could explain the crimes committed by his legions of murderers, but to no avail. Last we heard, he was CEO of Buchanan Renewables, a company producing biomass from unproductive rubber trees in Liberia. Even there, the retired colonel could not help being embroiled into controversy. His company was charged with corruption offenses by the Liberian legislature and was the subject of an investigation report published in 2011 by the Center for Research on Multinational Corporations. According to the report, Buchanan Renewables had a negative impact on the livelihoods of many smallholder farmers in Liberia. Steele is also registered with the Premiere Speakers Bureau, through which he charges $15,000 to deliver speeches on "security and counterterrorism policies."

Blackwater: An Army of Gangsters

It was a hot Sunday in Baghdad on September 16, 2007, but clouds were soon to cover the sky, so to speak. Four armored vehicles were driving slowly one behind the other near the Nisour Square, located in the Mansour District. A familiar sight for the citizens of the capital. Each of the vehicles was equipped with a submachine gun perched on its top and was carrying personnel from the private security firm Blackwater. All sons and husbands who, without knowing it, were going to cause one of the worst slaughters in the history of the second Iraq war. According to the Iraqi government account, as the first vehicle of the convoy was driving into Nisour Square, a Kia sedan approached the place but on the wrong side of the street, the driver ignoring a police officer's signal to drive away. At that very moment, the Blackwater team fired warning shots, then lethal shots at the Kia, before setting off stun grenades to clear the scene. The Iraqi police, mistaking the stun grenades for fragmentation grenades, opened fire at the Blackwater men, who responded right away to the attack. The American security company's version of the story, though, differs slightly. The Kia's driver, according to the official line, drove directly toward the convoy, ignoring verbal orders and hand signals. An Iraqi policeman then rushed to the car, but the latter kept moving forward. Thinking that it was a vehicle bomb and that the policeman was complicit, the Blackwater team began firing, killing the two people in the Kia as well as the policeman. In response, other Iraqi police officers retaliated, firing at the Blackwater convoy. The consequences of that fateful Sunday: 17 dead among Iraqis, 20 wounded, 15 cars damaged or destroyed. Following the incident, Blackwater news releases referred to a "violent attack" that its employees had been subjected to, claiming that these had acted "appropriately" and that they were true "heroes" who defended the lives of Americans in a war zone. It was not, however, Prime Minister Nouri al-Maliki's opinion. Al-Maliki described Blackwater's conduct as "criminal" and ordered its expulsion from Iraq, which did not happen until two years later.

Blackwater changed its name to Xe in 2009 and to Academi in 2011 after it was acquired by a group of investors. The firm was founded in 1997 by former Navy SEAL Officer Erik Prince, a strong supporter of the Republican Party. The new Academi owns an area of over 9 square miles in Moyock, North Carolina, south of the Norfolk Naval Base. Its activities began in military training, but following the shooting at Columbine High School in 1999, it obtained contracts with police academies for training in school interventions. In the aftermath of the October 2000 terrorist attacks against the USS Cole, a guided missile destroyer, Blackwater signed a $37 million contract with the U.S. Navy to train a protection force. But it was after 9/11 that the Moyock-based company became the flagship of the paramilitary industry. Blackwater was one of the first private military companies to set up shop in Afghanistan during the American intervention that started in October 2001. Despite being officially hired only for contracts relating to defensive actions, Blackwater nonetheless joined the CIA and special units in offensive raids. The contracts were easy to obtain since Erik Prince had close ties to members of the Bush administration, including Alvin Bernard Krongard, the number three at the CIA at the time. For instance, the agency entered into an agreement with Blackwater for the protection of the Baku-Tbilisi-Ceyhan pipeline, a huge deal that filled the pockets of Erik Prince. The firm secured many other contracts around the world, among others in Ukraine, and, of course, in Iraq.

The anger of the Iraqis reached a point of no return in the days following the Nisour Square massacre, all the more so since their frustration had been building up for four years. Four years during which Blackwater had been accumulating blunders with no ill effects for any of its employees. Like that time when, on Christmas Eve 2006, Andrew Moonen fired on one of Iraqi Vice President Adel Abdel-Mehdi's bodyguards, killing him instantly. Moonen, who had just left a party, was intoxicated. It was not long before he was evacuated to the United States, an evacuation requested by Washington, according to Blackwater officials. The firm's CEO, Erik Prince, later confirmed that he had fired Moonen and revoked his security clearance. The sanction, though, only lasted the time the former employee took to unpack because the Defense Department hired him just weeks after the incident for a "contract in the Middle East." The Homeland Security section of the Justice Department subsequently opened a criminal investigation against Moonen, but it was terminated by the U.S. Attorney's Office, which justified its decision by stating that there was "not sufficient evidence to obtain and sustain a conviction beyond a reasonable doubt." Moonen currently works for the Washington State Department of Corrections in the Special Offender Unit at the Monroe Correctional Complex.

A rehearsal of the Nisour Square scene occurred in May 2007 when Blackwater employees shot at a vehicle that had gotten a little too close to their convoy, according to them, killing its driver. A skirmish had ensued between the paramilitaries and the Iraqi police, which skirmish was caused by the culprits' refusal to give their identity and their version of the facts. The day before, the private security firm had been involved in a similar event that required the intervention of the American Army; four people had been killed. Another time, on February 7, 2007, a Blackwater sniper, positioned on the roof of the building housing the minister of Justice, killed an Iraqi guard who worked for the state-owned press agency *Al-Iraqiya*. The Iraqi government investigated the case and concluded that the sniper "opened fire [...] intentionally without any provocation." One last example: in May 2004, a Blackwater convoy transporting the spokesman of the American Ambassador to Baghdad, Robert J. Callahan, had fired on a taxi car, killing one of the passengers, a 19-year-old man. Many other such occurrences took place in the shadow of Blackwater, but under the direction of the Bush administration, the security firm never had to suffer the consequences of its actions. A report prepared by the Democratic representative Henry Waxman noted that from 2005 to 2007, Blackwater employees opened fire 195 times in Iraqi territory, and in the vast majority of cases, the paramilitaries had been the instigators of the shootings. These figures, however, come from the company's files. An ex-employee spoke of four to five incidents per week involving the Blackwater staff.

Erik Prince's company won contracts of over one billion dollars with the U.S. government, only in Iraq. One of these contracts, worth $27 million, was intended to provide security for Paul Bremer, the former head of the Coalition Provisional Authority. Bremer, for that matter, was very generous with his protectors: on June 27, 2004, he signed a decree called *Order 17*, which granted full immunity to private security firms in Iraq. In all, 170 of these security firms were, from then on, able to operate on Iraqi territory with impunity. But it was Blackwater that the Bush administration most thoroughly valued. The firm had such a special relationship with Bush and Co. that it enjoyed preferential treatment and almost absolute immunity long before Paul Bremer's decree. A preferential treatment that was renewed in December 2007, three months after the Nisour Square massacre, when Blackwater was looking for "security specialists" thanks to new contracts it had just signed with the State Department. Yet, it was bad timing to make new commitments with a company whose CEO was under the spotlight. On October 2, 2007, Erik Prince had been summoned to a hearing chaired by the House Committee on Oversight and Government Reform to answer questions from delegates about the conduct of Blackwater in Iraq and Afghanistan. Knowing that he would be facing a shower of blames and denunciations, the CEO had relied on the public relations firm BKSH & Associates Worldwide, the same that had represented the crook Ahmed Chalabi, the man behind the fake news regarding Saddam Hussein's weapons of mass destruction. When one of the congressmen asked Prince why Andrew Moonen had been evacuated from Iraq after the death of the Iraqi Vice President's bodyguard, Blackwater's number one had offered a sardonic answer: "We couldn't whip or incarcerate him", he said without emotion. In the end, BKSH & Associates Worldwide was of no help to its client: in December 2008, a study group from the State Department recommended that Blackwater be discarded as the main provider of private security services for American diplomats in Iraq. On January 30, 2009, Washington, then under the rule of a new president, announced that it was not renewing its contracts with the paramilitary organization.

Some saw in the behavior of the Blackwater employees a strong desire for revenge in response to an attack that had killed four of them in 2004 in Fallujah, where their bodies had even been mutilated and hung from a city bridge. Such a shock certainly left traces in their minds. That slaughter had plunged America into a mad rage, and the media had called for the death penalty against the "thugs" who had perpetrated this "crime of the century." Brigadier General Mark Kimmitt, a spokesman for the U.S. Army, had insisted: "[…] we will be back in Fallujah. It will be at the time and place of our choosing. We will hunt down the criminals." Kimmitt was right; as we have seen, that is precisely what happened later, but the Americans' response was more ruthless than expected.

In all press rooms in America, the main narrative described Blackwater employees as "civilian contractors" whose main task was to provide food to the Iraqis. It was as if they were associated with the Red Cross. What the journalists had forgotten to mention is that, as far as possible, no "civilian contractor" is empowered to carry a weapon and ride with armored vehicles.

Obama Opens the Door to the Syrian Jihad

At the end of 2011, Iraqi leaders claimed to be ready to take over the helm of their country. The message was heard in Washington, where President Barack Obama accepted this idea without batting an eye. The new occupant of the Oval Office, from that point forward, began to speak of Iraq as a "democratic" and "inclusive" country, adding that with its "enormous potential", it would undoubtedly get back on its feet very quickly. This was just any fable that would haunt the President until the end of his last mandate. Because in Iraq, things never go well. It is true the country has enormous potential, but democracy out there is slow to find a place in the sun. All it took for a storm to sweep through the country was for Prime Minister Nouri al-Maliki to go away from Baghdad for a few days. While in Washington to announce the transfer of power, al-Maliki received bad news directly from the Iraqi capital: his Vice President, the Sunni Tareq al-Hashemi, was planning a coup. These were at least the rumors flying around, and the Prime Minister relayed the information to Barack Obama. But the U.S. President had no intention to backtrack. For him, Iraq had to be turned over to the Iraqis. Al-Maliki took this position as a green light to crack down on the "plotters." The so-called coup was ultimately foiled, and al-Hashemi took refuge in Qatar, from where he pleaded his innocence. Subjected to torture, his bodyguards confessed that a plot to overthrow al-Maliki was indeed under preparation. But the latter could not sit idly by as he thought his government was at stake. Iraq was in dire need of a purge, according to him, a sure way to clean the political stables. Therefore, the Prime Minister, who is of Shiite origin one must remember, ordered the arrest of thousands of Sunnis who were accused of sedition. Several were imprisoned for days and months without access to a lawyer. Others were killed by James Steele's Shiite militias. The Sunnis, persecuted by a new power that sought revenge for the Saddam Hussein period, then thought it wise to revolt, frustrated that the situation had turned to their disadvantage. Granted, the rebellion was exacerbated by an unemployment rate hovering around 40%, but this did not alter the fact that the main problem was al-Maliki's government. James Jeffrey, the U.S. Ambassador to Iraq from 2010 to 2012, had warned the White House that the country's Prime Minister had to go, but Obama would not listen. One year away from the presidential elections and a possible second term, the President thought Iraq was too much of a thorn in the side of its American protectors. Better to get rid of this case as soon as possible. Yet, it should have been evident for the U.S. President that the new Iraqi government had messed things up. By the time the American troops were packing up to leave Iraq, the insurgency was reduced to nothing. But a handful of diehard activists joined forces with remaining members of Saddam Hussein's Republican Guard who had two major grievances: al-Maliki's purges, and the layoffs ordered by the American "invader." Abu Bakr al-Baghdadi was one of these diehard activists. The future leader helped around 500

Sunni prisoners escape from Iraqi jails. As a thank you, some of them formed with him the bulk of the first contingents of the Islamic State (ISIS). In Washington, officials expressed their concern about these events, but al-Maliki remained deaf to their calls, pretending he alone could solve the crisis. In some districts of Mosul, the presence of the former branch of Al-Qaeda—called "Islamic State" afterward—was met with positive reactions. With only 800 fighters, the jihadist group finally succeeded in conquering the entire city of Mosul, and later other major cities in northern Iraq, until it controlled much of the Iraqi territory. The pressure cranked up a notch within the U.S. political circle as ISIS threatened to enter Erbil, the capital of Kurdistan. With oil interests no stranger to the American awakening, Obama decided to send an air force to bomb the jihadist organization's positions. The second Iraqi conflict of the 21st century had just begun.

Iraq was not the only problem the Obama administration was facing. On the other side of the border, in Syria, the Islamic State had taken over a few major cities as well. As soon as August 2011, Abu Bakr al-Baghdadi sent militants to Syria to recruit jihadists against al-Assad. Those jihadists created the Al-Nusra Front, the Syrian branch of Al-Qaeda. The official IS-Front merger occurred on April 8, 2013, a merger that the Al-Qaeda HQ never agreed to. The rise of the Islamic State, which, from then on, had become independent, was to take a major turning point on June 29, 2014, when al-Baghdadi declared himself commander of the believers, that is, the highest authority in the Muslim world. But three years earlier, the start of another conflict had caught the eyes of American leaders.

THE DARK SIDE OF THE INTERVENTION IN LIBYA

For four decades, Muammar Gaddafi paraded in front of the cameras with world leaders, among whom Western political figures. But in spring 2011, those Western political figures threatened to drive him out of power, a project put forward first by the government of Nicolas Sarkozy in France, then by UK's David Cameron, and finally by Barack Obama. After the overthrow of the dictator, Libya, whose cultural heritage has never given room for democracy, quickly fell into chaos. Today, two governments are ruling the country, large parts of which are even controlled by the Tuareg and Tubu peoples. What happened in Libya equally happened in Iraq and would have happened in Syria as well if President Bashar al-Assad had been brought down. This part of the world, the Levant, is nothing but a powder keg, and the desire to topple governments has more to do with a willingness to embrace the power and/or promote geopolitical interests than with the sake of improving the fate of peoples. Despite the repeated failures of regime changes, many political analysts still believe that everything is possible, that resorting to a discourse alluding to the Age of Enlightenment will turn the international community into a liberal ground. If such a thing were easy, we would probably be ruled by a world government whose states would constitute affiliated federations, which is far from being the case.

The United States hit a wall in Iraq. A huge wall of opposition against an intervention based on deception, but also a wall of hatred, which was poured out on Western values, the main victims of this showdown. The truth is, America and its allies faced a counter-offensive in Iraq that showed all the contempt that the Islamists can generate toward the political system on which these values are based. Yet, it did not occur to American leaders that the Iraqi failure could prove to be a forerunner of the Libyan and Syrian failures. It was a serious mistake. Thousands of dead soldiers and civilians, as well as billions of dollars allocated to the reconstruction of Iraq and Libya are too many proofs of this reality. The liberal media, for their part, have not yet understood—or perhaps they pretend to ignore—that financial and geopolitical interests still take precedence over political virtue. That is why the observer who relies on a literal reading of the media coverage of the Middle East conflicts can barely grasp the mechanisms underlying the phenomenon. Behind-the-scenes games are unfortunately the driving force of politics. Without them, any decision would be vulnerable to public opinion, which would prompt governments to be too cautious in their interventions, a tactic that cannot work in hyperactive states at the international level because prudent politicians are too often unable to protect their country's geopolitical interests. Rivalries and power struggles, arms sales, and the confiscation of wealth cannot operate freely in a system strangled by restraint and moderation. One thus understands why the Middle East is in perpetual conflict and why many authors write books like this one, because in a global world where governments did not subscribe to any geopolitical logic, these same authors would certainly put their pencils away for lack of subjects.

The First Signs

In 2011, the Arab Spring signed the death warrant of a handful of regimes in the Middle East, namely the government of Hosni Mubarak in Egypt, Zine el-Abidine Ben Ali in Tunisia, and Ali Abdallah Saleh in Yemen. All three followed the same path as Gaddafi's Libya, a path that Bashar al-Assad's Syria should also have taken, but it rather survived at the cost of great efforts and thousands of deaths caused by a never-ending civil war. Muammar Gaddafi was used to rebellions and opposition movements, going through at least three assassination attempts during his reign. Therefore, the first protests of January 13, 2011, came as no surprise to him and his entourage. During the troubled times which led to his fall, the sixty-something dictator showed two faces: that of the bloodthirsty tyrant who wanted to maintain power with guns and batons, and that of the conciliator, sometimes opportunistic, a side of his personality the Western media preferred to hide. Whether or not he was serious in his approach, the former Libyan leader tried to defuse the situation from the outset by proposing *ad hoc* measures: abolition of taxes and customs duties on food, special premiums for families, creation of a $24 billion fund to develop the country and provide housing. On February 16, the dictator released 110 Islamist prisoners at the very moment when his son Saif al-Islam, the successor in title, promised political reforms. In early April, the tone within the Gaddafi clan became more and more conciliatory as Tripoli put forward the idea of holding referendums aiming at the establishment of democracy. The countries of the coalition, with the United Kingdom, France and the United States leading the charge, saw these proposals as a good start to resolve the crisis, but the Libyan opposition rejected them all, an opposition that had just opened the door to Al-Qaeda fighters, as the Western chancelleries would soon discover. In politics, however, the wind can quickly change direction, and this is exactly what happened on April 30 when the Libyan dictator's youngest son, Saif al-Arab Gaddafi, and three of his grandchildren were killed during a NATO bombing without the international community showing any particular concern. On June 16, Saif al-Islam proposed new concessions: the holding of free elections under international supervision, and the withdrawal of his father should he lose his seat. But the call came too late since the goal of the coalition was already set: Gaddafi had to go. Its wish will be granted in October with the death of the dictator, who managed, despite everything, to run his country for 42 years.

UK's Jihadists

On May 22, 2017, Salman Ramadan Abedi blew himself up just after an Ariana Grande concert in Manchester, a stronghold of the United Kingdom's Libyan diaspora. The toll was heavy: 23 dead and 139 wounded; several hundred more suffered psychological trauma. It was the largest terrorist attack to strike the British territory since the July 7, 2005, London bombings. Salman Ramadan Abedi was the second child of a Libyan refugee couple who fled the Gaddafi regime. More importantly, he was linked to an organization that Her Majesty's foreign intelligence service, the MI6, knew very well: the Libyan Islamic Fighting Group (LIFG). In the United States as in the United Kingdom, the LIFG is considered a terrorist entity. But despite that designation, the group was, until not too long ago, tolerated in the UK, where, hunted down in Libya by Gaddafi's intelligence services, some of its members relocated, knowing that they would be welcomed in that country so compassionate toward the "persecuted." Other LIFG members—and there were many—preferred to swell the ranks of Al-Qaeda in Afghanistan. Among them: Anas al-Libi, one of the organizers of the 1998 attacks on the American embassies in Dar es Salaam, Tanzania, and Nairobi, Kenya; Ibn al-Sheikh al-Libi, to whom Al-Qaeda had assigned the command of a training camp in Afghanistan; and Abu Hafs al-Libi, who had served in Iraq alongside Abu Musab al-Zarqawi. One of the LIFG leaders, Abdelhakim Belhaj, had maintained close ties with the ex-leader of the Afghan Taliban, Mullah Omar, as well as with senior Al-Qaeda members.

Salman Ramadan Abedi had been reported five times to the British authorities before he committed his crime, and the FBI had even placed him on its watch list in 2016. Greatly influenced by the Islamic State, the young man had joined one of the terrorist group's cells operating in the south of Manchester. He took his first steps in jihad in 2011 when the revolt was in full swing in Libya. He and his father traveled to this country to take part in the events that led to a regime change in October. Abedi was only 16 at the time, so it is unlikely that he fought, but that is not what matters. Because if there is one thing to remember, it is that both the father and the son went to Libya with the tacit consent of the MI6, according to sources within the Libyan diaspora. To better understand the collaboration that existed between the LIFG and the British government, we have to go back to 1995.

The following story was told by a former MI5 (the domestic intelligence branch) officer, David Shayler, but it is worth mentioning that it has not been confirmed by mainstream media sources. Shayler said that he had heard from a coworker that an official from the Libyan services had turned up in 1995 at the British Embassy in Tunis, Tunisia, to speak with the MI6 representative. The subject: a coup d'état, paired with the assassination of President Gaddafi. The Libyan, whose code name was "Tunworth", asked the MI6 officer the following question: would Her Majesty's government be ready to finance these two projects? The answer came later, and if we are to believe David Shayler, it had been a positive one. In return for the MI6 support, "Tunworth" is said to have offered to turn over the two Libyan suspects in the 1988 bombings of the Pan Am flight 103 that caused the crash of a Boeing 747 in Lockerbie, Scotland, killing all 243 passengers and 16 crew. The British investigation had uncovered a plot led by Gaddafi's government. David Watson, an MI6 officer who allegedly acted as an intermediary between "Tunworth" and the intelligence service, handed over the equivalent of $40,000 to his informant during a meeting in Geneva. The plan, though, never worked: in February 1996, Gaddafi was the target of an assassination attempt in Sirte but he escaped unharmed. The conspirators have reportedly received about $160,000 from the MI6, according to David Shayler. All were members of the Libyan Islamic Fighting Group. A confidential report from the French Directorate General for External Security (Direction générale de la sécurité extérieure-DGSE) seems in part to support David Shayler's story about the "deal" that had been made between the MI6 and jihadists, among others the LIFG. According to the report, written between July 2000 and October 2001, the CIA and the MI6 allowed—directly or indirectly—Ibn al-Sheikh al-Libi, a former LIFG member, to control the operations of an Al-Qaeda training camp in Darunta, Afghanistan, until 1995. A note within the report reveals that the "training in

Darunta [...] focused on the manufacturing and use of explosives [...]. This training, initially provided at the Khalden camp, in the province of Paktiyâ, was shifted in 1995 to Darunta upon a directive from [Ibn al-Sheikh al-Libi] in order to transfer control from the hands of the security services of certain countries, notably the United States and the United Kingdom", to Al-Qaeda. After the terrorist group took control of Darunta, the camp was used to prepare its members for a series of deadly attacks, including those of August 1998 at two American embassies in Africa. This note from the DGSE report, it must be said, was made public by the online blogger and journalist Wayne Madsen. The author of the book you are currently reading wishes to stress that he has never read the original note in French.

Following the attacks of September 11, 2001, the tone changed dramatically in the offices of the British Parliament, and Gaddafi suddenly became a prominent figure in London. For the man, who wished to ingratiate himself with the Westerners—he mostly feared American airstrikes on his country—, was then promoting unity and reconciliation, as much as he was promising to put an end to his nuclear program. But if the dictator got promoted in London, his enemies, among them the LIFG, were elevated to the rank of first-class outlaws. As a consequence, close cooperation gradually developed between the MI6 and the Libyan services. Moussa Koussa, former Libya's foreign intelligence chief under Gaddafi, provided information to the CIA and the MI6 on LIFG agents who had trained in Al-Qaeda camps in Afghanistan and on those who were active within the British soil. The list of these was quite long: 79 militants opposed to Gaddafi were living in the United Kingdom at that time. The MI6 did not take long to respond by helping the Libyan services to kidnap some of these opponents, sometimes with the assistance of allies. This was the case of two officials from the Libyan Islamic Fighting Group: Abdel Hakim Belhaj, the head of the military command, and Sami al-Saadi, its spiritual leader. Belhaj and his wife, Fatima Bouchar, then 4 months pregnant, were in Beijing and about to board a plane bound for London when they were apprehended by the Chinese authorities. Deported to Malaysia where they were detained for a time, the two Libyans were subsequently sent over to Bangkok. On March 6, 2004, a CIA fax was relayed to the Libyan services: "We are planning to take control of the pair in Bangkok and place them on our aircraft for a flight to your country", the message said. The same evening, the Malaysian authorities brought the two Libyans up on a flight to Bangkok. In the Thai capital, they were taken off the aircraft and transferred to a CIA detention center located inside Don Mueang Airport. In his testimony, Belhaj stated that he was beaten and hung from hooks at the detention center. His wife, Fatima Bouchar, was chained down to a wall and subjected to a zero-calorie diet for five days. The couple was finally moved to Tripoli and Belhaj imprisoned in Tadjourah, where he was once again chained and beaten by the Qaddafi jailers. He spent six years in prison. As for Sami al-Saadi, he was not living in UK but in Tehran with his wife and four children when the MI6 managed to intercept his phone calls. The UK's intelligence service then passed the information on to the Libyans. In March 2004, the British, working on behalf of the Gaddafi regime, deceived al-Saadi into believing that he could be provided with asylum in the United Kingdom, so the two parties agreed to a meeting in Hong Kong to talk about this offer. The LIFG's spiritual leader and his family then traveled to the Asian metropolis, convinced that British diplomats were waiting for them to confirm the good news. It was a bad move: the clan was taken into custody by the Hong Kong authorities and extradited to Libya. Like Belhaj, al-Saadi was locked up and beaten in Gaddafi's prisons.

The relations between the Libyans and the British were more than harmonious at the time. The MI6 director, Mark Allen, and his Libyan counterpart, Moussa Koussa, became good friends, going so far as to exchange gifts and birthday wishes. The first had even invited the second to a banquet on September 20, 2003, at the luxurious Goring Hotel in London, to celebrate the first anniversary of their initial meeting. Perhaps the MI6 chief had forgotten—or was never made aware of—Koussa's statements, reported in June 1980 in *The Times*, in which he confessed to having authorized the assassination of two Libyan residents in the United Kingdom. Perhaps Allen had also forgotten the ten bomb attacks perpetrated in Manchester and London against opponents of the Gaddafi government, attacks that, led by Koussa, had left 29 wounded. None of those affairs had obviously been discussed at the famous banquet in September 2003. It is also the same Koussa who had been photographed with a "great lady", Hillary Clinton, when he visited the White House. It was in 2010, and both were flashing a beaming smile in front of the cameras. After all, folks in Washington quickly change sides. Prime Minister Tony Blair, too, seemed to have wiped the slate clean when, in October 2002, he wrote a letter to Gaddafi in which he proposed to lift the sanctions that hung over Libya's oil industry. In return, Tripoli was ordered to give up its nuclear weapons program. Pleased with this open-door policy, the dictator assured the Prime Minister of his full cooperation. Yet, a year later, a cargo ship flying the flag of Germany was intercepted in the Italian port of Taranto, where a search enabled the Italian authorities to confiscate parts used to make centrifuges. The parts in question had been loaded in Malaysia and were to be shipped to factories in Libya. Under pressure, the Gaddafi government had no choice but to accept the dismantling of its nuclear program. It was a step in the right direction for Prime Minister Tony Blair who visited Tripoli on March 25, 2004, shaking hands with the Libyan dictator in front of reporters delighted to show those images to their viewers. Two days after the meeting, the British government began the process of extraordinary rendition of Sami al-Saadi, the Libyan Islamic Fighting Group's spiritual leader. Coincidentally or not, it was then announced in London that Shell, the Anglo-Dutch company, had just signed a £110 million contract to obtain the rights for oil exploration off the Libyan coast. In fact, 122 companies had been able to register to apply for oil and gas exploration permits in that area, and several of them benefited from the same privilege as Shell. According to Tarek Hassan-Beck, a senior executive at the National Oil Corporation (NOC), of the 122 companies, 63 were given the green light to submit bids. Let's say it clearly: Blair's open-door policy was just another strategy to make it possible for British companies to accumulate profits.

In 2011, the United Kingdom witnessed another dramatic turn of events: the government, once again, changed its mind and decided this time to oppose Gaddafi. No more partying with Libyan crooks, everyone, from then on, had to be clean at Downing Street. And since the LIFG also opposed the Libyan dictator, it thus found itself on the "right" side of the fence, even though the organization had a long history of collaboration with Al-Qaeda not only in Afghanistan but also in Iraq after the American intervention. As if this were not enough, the LIFG had teamed up with the Moroccan Islamic Fighting Group in five synchronized suicide bombings that left 45 people dead in Casablanca, Morocco, in May 2003. This event alone should have dissuaded London from hooking up with the LIFG. On the contrary, the MI6, as we have seen, authorized members and supporters of that organization to join the ranks of the rebels in Libya. The British government's determination to do away with Gaddafi was such that those exiles, some of whom were listed in intelligence records, were able to take back their passports and, as a bonus, underwent military training sponsored by Her Majesty's Special Air Service (SAS). As it happens, dozens of Special Forces soldiers and MI6 officers were already at work inside Libya in March 2011. General David Richards, then-Chief of the Defense Staff, said that Britain "had a few people embedded" with the rebel forces and that they were "going forward and back" in the rear areas. Ironically, a special forces unit was captured the same month near Benghazi by rebels who did not know who they were dealing with. A senior official of the local revolutionary council said about it: "They were carrying espionage equipment, reconnaissance equipment, multiple passports and weapons." At that time, however, Prime Minister Cameron was repeating the same message: there is no question of overthrowing Gaddafi. A message that had found an echo in Washington.

In all these scenes of political acrobatics, we must not forget a precious ally of the Americans and the British, Qatar, which stood on the front line to defend the cause of the rebels. The tiny Gulf principality, whose longtime ambition is to replace Saudi Arabia as the region's leader, provided $400 million to Libyan opposition forces, but much of this money fell into the hands of Islamist radicals. Qatar's favorite organization was the February 17th Martyrs Brigade, to which it secretly transferred anti-tank weapons, among other things. The brigade was led by a well-known figure: Abdel Hakim Belhaj, the same man who was once the military leader of the Libyan Islamic Fighting Group. Belhaj commanded his troops in the Libyan capital, Tripoli. The United States was very pleased to have found a sponsor and supplier of weapons to the rebels, a situation that allowed Uncle Sam to remain in the shadows, at least for a while. It was not long, however, before the White House received disturbing reports: lots of Qatari weapons were landing in the hands of not only the February 17th Martyrs Brigade but also of more radical jihadist groups. As we stressed before, the Americans rarely learn from their experiences, and barely a year later, they woke up in Syria with the same thorny problem. Abdel-Hakim al-Hasidi, a Libyan who headed up security under the NATO-backed National Transitional Council in the city of Derna, had pointed out the extremist character of the rebels supported by the coalition in Libya. Al-Hasidi had claimed that the Libyans who had fought with Al-Qaeda against American forces in Iraq had returned to topple Gaddafi, adding that these fighters "[were] patriots and good Muslims, not terrorists", but that members of Al-Qaeda "[were] also good Muslims and fighting against the invader." It should be recalled, after reading these words, that al-Hasidi was in charge of a NATO-backed security service. That is how things were going on in Libya during the Arab Spring.

Hillary Clinton on the Front Line

Many blamed the United States for supporting Islamist opponents in Syria, but surprisingly, they remained silent while the same scenario played out a few months earlier in Libya. Saif al-Islam Gaddafi, the dictator's son and heir, had warned the tenants of the White House against the rebels who opposed his father. Those, he had trumpeted, were Islamists, even "gangsters and terrorists", before being freedom fighters, as they were called in Western circles. "And now you have NATO supporting them with ships, planes, helicopters, weapons [and] training [...]", he had said in a conversation with an American official. But why should anybody listen to the son of the new enemy? Convinced that his government was blameless, Saif al-Islam had asked

Washington to send a team of observers to his country to see for itself that the situation was different from the one depicted in the Western media. That invitation had come with a guarantee that the regime had no intention of harming its citizens. Al-Islam rightly feared that Secretary of State Hillary Clinton was seeking a pretext for ousting his father. He had even compared Clinton's smear campaign to the Bush administration's false accusations against Saddam Hussein that the former Iraqi president had weapons of mass destruction in his possession, a ploy that Bush had used to pressure the Congress so the U.S. could invade Iraq. The son had indeed a thousand and one reasons to assume the worst. Hillary Clinton kept claiming that Gaddafi was planning to commit genocide against civilians in Benghazi, where the rebels had set up their quarters. An idea that neither the Secretary of Defense Robert Gates nor the Chairman of the Joint Chiefs of Staff Admiral Michael Mullen, both fiercely opposed to the use of force against Gaddafi, supported. And if these two officials rejected the Secretary of State's position on the matter, it was because the U.S. military intelligence services had found no evidence suggesting that the Libyan state was about to carry out a mass killing. Mullen's deputy, General Charles H. Jacoby Jr., had made it clear that he did not trust the reports coming out of the State Department and the CIA, but that he could not do anything about it. The Pentagon leaders sensed that their hands were tied precisely because Hillary Clinton, sidestepping her colleague at the Defense Department, had urged them to stop all communication with Gaddafi's entourage. But the generals had overruled this order and stayed in touch with the Libyan government, at least behind the scenes. And these "four stars" had at least one ally in the Congress: the Democratic representative Dennis J. Kucinich of Ohio, who had sent a letter to Hillary Clinton and President Obama after speaking on the phone with Saif al-Islam. In his letter, Kucinich argued that cooperation between the U.S. and Libya was necessary since the latter was willing to negotiate an agreement to end the conflict. That was exactly what the generals were trying to explain to the hawks in Washington. But neither the Oval Office nor the State Department responded to Kucinich's letter. A Gaddafi confidant, Mohammed Ismael, had spoken at the same time with Gene Cretz, former U.S. Ambassador to

Libya, and had confirmed to him that the senior officers of the Libyan Army had been ordered not to shoot the demonstrators. Cretz had, in a way, become the intermediary between the American government and its Libyan counterpart, or, if you will, the U.S.'s main henchman in the official channel that had been set up with Libya, a channel that, however, turned out to be but a facade, a sort of avenue that was useful to Washington to save time before embarking on a campaign whose ultimate goal was the overthrow of Gaddafi. Which campaign enabled the State Department to hide under the cover of United Nations Security Council resolution 1973, adopted on March 17, 2011, and that formed the legal basis for military intervention in the Libyan Civil War. The resolution demanded "an immediate ceasefire", but also authorized the international community to establish a no-fly zone and to use all means necessary to protect civilians in Libya. Four days later, in a speech to the British Parliament, Prime Minister David Cameron declared that it was not his intentions to promote a regime change in Gaddafi's country. A point of view shared by his American equal, Barack Obama, during a speech to the nation: "The task I have assigned our forces [is] to protect the Libyan people from immediate danger, and to establish a no-fly zone [...]", he said, adding that "broadening our military mission to include regime change would be a mistake." These proved to be pure lies, though, because on March 19, a British airstrike showed all the features of an act of war: 110 Tomahawks cruise missiles, launched from a British submarine stationed in the Mediterranean Sea, struck around twenty Libyan targets, including an administrative center belonging to the Libyan government in Bab al-Azizia, located near the dictator's residence. A few hours after these strikes, Vice Admiral William E. Gortney said with full seriousness, in front of servile journalists, that Muammar Gaddafi and his family were not on the list of potential targets. Perhaps they were not, but the fact remains that in the following weeks, a NATO airstrike killed a son of Gaddafi and three of his grandchildren in the family compound in Tripoli. And this type of intervention increased exponentially until the abdication of the regime and the death of its leader in October. In fact, on October 20, a U.S. Predator drone and a French fighter attacked the convoy in which the dictator was trying to flee the city of Sirte. The latter was wounded and captured before being killed by the rebels.

In addition to implementing a no-fly zone, the 1973 UN resolution strengthened the arms embargo imposed by the previous resolution 1970. On April 19, a U.S. brigadier general took up the issue, declaring that no embargo violation had been reported until then. An army spokesman had followed suit and stated on May 13 that there was nothing to suggest that weapons were being transferred to the rebels. Again, officials tried to hide a reality that would blow up right in their face a few months later. Arms stocks belonging to the Libyan government were regularly stolen during the crisis and several fell into the hands of Islamist militias, including the Nigerian terrorist group Boko Haram and what would become the Islamic State. In January 2014, one of these militias shot down an Egyptian helicopter using a portable missile system that had been taken out of Gaddafi's stockpile. It was also known that Qatar had delivered French-made Milan missiles to the rebels and that it had not cared about who were the recipients. Crew members of a Canadian frigate, the HMCS Charlottetown, had intercepted arms shipments on a ship owned by opposition groups, but when the frigate's captain had contacted the NATO HQ to obtain instructions, he had been told to turn back and let the ship take its course. Embargo you said?

The hellish trio, namely the United States, France and the United Kingdom, was asking for war and got it. The go-betweens appointed by the Pentagon, who had established their own channels of discussion with Gaddafi, did everything to find a solution to the crisis, but the White House closed the doors to any possible resolution. In late March, at the height of the storm, Charles R. Kubic, a retired U.S. Navy Rear Admiral who was working in Libya as a consultant, had been approached by senior military officials from the Gaddafi regime to propose a 72-hour truce. Kubic had then spoken about that matter to Lieutenant Colonel Brian Linvill of the U.S. African Command (AFRICOM), who, in turn, had passed the proposal on to General Carter Ham, AFRICOM's commander-in-chief. According to Kubic, the Libyans were ready to end the military operations and move their troops to the outskirts of some of Libya's main cities, where they would take on a defensive role. They were equally willing to allow African Union envoys to guarantee that the truce is respected. But there was more: "[Gaddafi] came back and said he was willing to step down and permit a transition government, but he had two conditions", said the Rear Admiral. "First was to [ensure] there was a military force left over after he left Libya capable [of going] after Al-Qaeda. Secondly, he wanted to have the sanctions against him and his family and those loyal to him lifted, and free passage. At that point in time, everybody thought that was reasonable." But this was not the opinion prevailing within the State Department, ruled with an iron fist by Hillary Clinton. General Ham was ordered to withdraw two days after the start of the negotiations with the Libyans. The order came from Clinton's office. What is ironic is that at first, the former Secretary of State was not convinced of the need to intervene in Libya, but it was before she met an opponent of the Gaddafi regime, Mahmoud Jibril, at the Westin Hotel in Paris, in mid-March 2011. Jibril was considered a moderate in Washington, Paris and London, which is why he had become the official political representative of the Libyan opposition within the National Transitional Council. The man had just resigned as head of the National Planning Council and of the National Economic Development Board in the Gaddafi government. Since his resignation, he had the habit of strutting around the Western world's major capitals to convince American and European leaders to support the Libyan revolt. Officially, Jibril said out loud that he wished for the advent of a democratic state in a new Libya, but he was more cautious when addressing Islamists, recalling that the Sharia law should be "the main reference in the drafting of the Libyan [future] constitution." That said, forty-five minutes after meeting with Jibril, Clinton announced that a military intervention in Libya was henceforth necessary. It is then that she forbade all contact with Saif al-Islam Gaddafi, even though his government had ordered a ceasefire, which the State Department firmly rejected.

The post-Gaddafi period has proven not to be an easy one for the new Libyan government and the Western leaders who wanted war.

Jeffrey D. Feltman, a former senior official in the State Department for the Middle East affairs, had expressed his concern about the situation in a lengthy email sent to Hillary Clinton. Feltman felt that Libya's interim leaders seemed completely disengaged. Mahmoud Jibril, the new Prime Minister who had talked Clinton into intervening against Gaddafi, "was commuting from Qatar, making only 'cameo' appearances in Libya", according to Feltman, who had also said that Islamists were planning to seize power, helped financially by members of the anti-Gaddafi coalition, notably Qatar. The former State Department official went on to add that after decades in exile, some leaders "were more familiar with American and European universities than with Libyan tribes and the militias that had sprung from them." Others, like Jibril, were seen with suspicion in certain circles because of their previous roles alongside Gaddafi. It was therefore increasingly evident that "the ragtag populist army that had actually done the fighting against Colonel Qaddafi was not taking orders from the men in suits who believed they were Libya's new leaders." In short, the sky was darkening over Libya, as it had darkened over Iraq years before.

Benghazi and the Sinking of the State Department

At around 9:40 p.m. on September 11, 2012, about sixty insurgents attacked the American consulate in Benghazi, Libya, causing the death of U.S. Ambassador J. Christopher Stevens and U.S. Foreign Service Information Management Officer Sean Smith. Stevens was the first American ambassador to be killed in the performance of his duties since 1979. Next, at around 4:00 a.m., the insurgents launched another attack, this time against a CIA annex located at approximately one mile away from the diplomatic compound, killing two paramilitaries, Tyrone S. Woods and Glen Doherty. Inside the consulate, an agent of the Diplomatic Security Service (DSS) reacted promptly to the attack and set off the alarm after seeing, from the security cameras, "a large number of men, armed men, flowing into the compound." Staff members grabbed the phone to call the Embassy in Tripoli, the Diplomatic Security Command Center in Washington, the headquarters of the February 17th Martyrs Brigade, which had been hired to guard the premises, and a quick reaction force based in the CIA annex. Ambassador Stevens himself called the deputy chief of the American mission in Libya, Gregory Hicks, whose quarters were in Tripoli, to inform him that the consulate was under attack. In the hours that followed, U.S. officials first described the assault as a mere demonstration in response to an "anti-Muslim" online video titled *Innocence of Muslims*. But further investigations showed that the operation was, on the contrary, premeditated, as we will see later. Sources quoted by *Fox News* stated that men from Ansar al-Sharia, one of the organizations responsible for the attack, had moved near the U.S. consulate a few weeks before the night of horror. Concerned neighbors had made requests to the authorities to improve security in the neighborhood, to no avail. "We warned [the Americans] against the guys who settled next door, but [...] nothing was done", said one of the locals. According to an intelligence source, the security personnel had repeatedly asked for an M240 machine gun to be mounted on the roof of the consulate to ensure better protection of the facility, but each time, Washington, more particularly Hillary Clinton's State Department, had denied the request. The latter waited almost a year and a half to place Ansar al-Sharia on the list of terrorist entities. Clinton, for that matter, was widely criticized for her lack of interest in the security of the consulate, located in one of the most unsafe cities in Libya at the time of the Arab Spring. Before the tragic events, the State Department had received several intelligence reports pointing out the fact that Al-Qaeda was maintaining a strong presence in the region and that the life of Ambassador Stevens was in danger. Diplomats on-site, including the former ambassador, had many times pleaded with the department to improve the security of the premises, without winning their case. Five scenarios had been proposed in this regard, but all had been turned down by the Clinton clan. Worse still, internal memos, revealed by *Fox News*, show that Undersecretary of State for Management, Patrick Francis Kennedy, had recommended that the Benghazi special mission be exempt from the State Department's physical security guidelines.

One of the intelligence reports made available to the State Department contained photographs identifying more than 300 Al-Qaeda members taking part in a demonstration in downtown Benghazi, less than a mile from the diplomatic outpost. The report outlined a quote from an Al-Qaeda leader in Benghazi who had clearly warned the United States that if they did not remove their chips from the Libyan table, his organization would take physical action against the ambassador. In Washington, the remark, apparently, did not raise eyebrows. Those statements did not come as a surprise. According to *The Telegraph* newspaper, the Al-Qaeda flag had "been spotted flying over the Benghazi Courthouse [...] next to the Libyan national flag." On June 18, 2012, in a daily intelligence report titled *Terrorism: Conditions Ripe for More Attacks, Terrorist Safe Haven in Libya*, the joint staff wrote: "[...] support will increase Libyan terrorist capability in the permissive post-revolution security environment. Attacks will also increase in number and lethality as terrorists connect with [Al-Qaeda] in Libya." On July 6, another note, this one from the CIA and similar to the preceding one, had also served as a warning: "Al-Qaeda-affiliated-groups and associates are exploiting the permissive security environment in Libya to enhance their capabilities and expand their operational reach." It was also mentioned in that note that Al-Qaeda in the Islamic Maghreb (AQIM) and Al-Qaeda in the Arabian Peninsula (AQPA) "have conducted training, built communication networks, and facilitated extremist travel across North Africa from their safe haven in parts of eastern Libya." On August 19, the Joint Staff published a second pessimistic note titled *(U) Libya: Terrorists to Increase Strength During Next Six Months*, in which it stressed that there was no indication to believe that the situation had changed in Libya, where the terrorists had increased their presence. At around the same time, the Benghazi mission had seen fit to call an emergency meeting due to Al-Qaeda's operations in the area. In a cable marked "secret", the local State Department's Regional Security Officer (RSO) had expressed his doubts about the protection of the consulate in the event of an attack. Finally, on September 5, AFRICOM produced a new analytical report that echoed the same warnings.

The U.S. Senate Select Committee on Intelligence, which investigated the events in Benghazi, had concluded, among other things, that the intelligence services had gleaned enough information to foresee a major attack against U.S. personnel in Benghazi. The local RSO alone had "compiled a list of 234 security incidents in Libya between June 2011 and July 2012, 50 of which took place in Benghazi." On the very day of the attacks, two security agents at the consulate had spotted a Libyan police officer taking pictures of the compound using his cell phone from a nearby building under construction. The man had been briefly put into custody before being released. In his diary, later found in the rubble of the compound, Ambassador Stevens had himself expressed his fear concerning the growing presence of Al-Qaeda in the region. The consulate was guarded by five armed security officers, three members of the February 17th Martyrs Brigade, a few officers of the Libyan national police, and five unarmed members of the Blue Mountain Group, a security firm. These men were no match for the sixty insurgents who launched the attack on the compound. Despite the risks, no significant measure, as we mentioned earlier, had been taken by the State Department to increase the security of the premises before September 11, 2012. Additional surveillance cameras were to be installed, but the bureaucrats waited too long before taking action. Yet, if there was one place that should have been closely monitored, it was the Benghazi consulate. Too many people and groups were showing—and are still showing—antipathy toward the United States for a thousand and one reasons. In April 2012, two individuals, who had once worked as security officers at the consulate, had thrown an improvised explosive device on the fence facing the compound. No one had been killed in the incident. Four days later, a similar device was thrown on a convoy of four vehicles carrying the United Nations Special Envoy to Libya. The bomb had exploded just over ten feet from the vehicle in which the official was traveling, without hurting anyone. On June 6, 2012, an Al-Qaeda-affiliated organization known as the "Brigades of the Imprisoned Sheikh Omar Abdel Rahman" had posted a video showing an attack with an explosive device outside the gates of the consulate; no casualties had resulted from it. A month earlier, the same brigades had claimed responsibility for an attack on the International Red Cross (ICRC) office in Benghazi, in response, they said, to the assassination of Abu Yahya al-Libi, a Libyan leader of Al-Qaeda who had just been killed by an American drone. On August 6, the ICRC finally decided to suspend its activities in Benghazi, a city deemed too dangerous for the organization. On June 10, the British Ambassador to Libya, Dominic Asquith, had survived an assassination attempt also in Benghazi. Two British police officers had been injured during the assault when their convoy was hit by a grenade. As a result, the Foreign Office had settled on a withdrawal of all consular staff from the city at the end of June.

For a while, the Obama administration maintained its false rhetoric that Al-Qaeda had been defeated and, therefore, that it could not be held responsible for the attacks in Benghazi. The "resistance" came mainly from the State Department, which was given a severe reprimand from the Senate for not being fully cooperative in its investigation. Aside from Hillary Clinton, Charlene Lamb, Deputy Assistant Secretary for International Programs in the Bureau of Diplomatic Security at the State Department, was the one the media was mostly focused on. Lamb, after all, was to blame for the multiple refusals that came from her department concerning the security of the Benghazi compound. She had, among other things, justified her position by arguing that it would have been very embarrassing for the United States if the Benghazi consulate's staff had been more significant than in the embassies of Pakistan and Yemen. An opinion that she surely regretted afterwards.

An Attack That Bears Al-Qaeda's Signature

Before the attack of September 11, 2012, the smell of Al-Qaeda had long been floating in the air of Benghazi, as we have seen. Yet, in Washington, the order was to tell the media that the attackers, although not being saints, had no connection to terrorism. It was repeated on every media platform that the assault had been spontaneous while all indications pointed to the mark of jihad. At least one official had resisted this attempt to manipulate information. The Libyan President Mohamed Yusuf Al Magariaf had put a lot of energy into emphasizing his opposition to the view held by the Obama administration: "The idea that this criminal and cowardly act was a spontaneous protest that just spun out of control is completely unfounded and preposterous", he had said in an interview with *NPR*. "We firmly believe that this was a precalculated, preplanned attack that was carried out specifically to attack the U.S. Consulate." As Saïf al-Islam Gaddafi had stated a year before, the rebels who opposed his father were "gangsters and terrorists", but "gangsters and terrorists" who, one should have noted, opposed the United States above all. In public, Washington preferred to remain silent about this reality, but things were quite different in private. The American activist group Judicial Watch got hold of "secret" documents from both the Defense and the State Departments that clearly show that these had known very early that the attack on the consulate had been planned by elements of Al-Qaeda. A note from the Defense Intelligence Agency (DIA), dated September 12, 2012, therefore the day after the attack, mentioned that the attackers wanted to "kill as many Americans as possible" and that the act had been carried out in response to the assassination of Abu Yahya al-Libi, a Libyan leader within Al-Qaeda. This was the same motive the Brigades of the Imprisoned Sheikh Omar Abdel Rahman, which had previously attacked the offices of the Red Cross in Benghazi in May 2012, had referred to. It was also on September 12 that Secretary of State Hillary Clinton, in a phone conversation with the Libyan Prime Minister Hesham Kandil, had said: "We know the attack in Libya had nothing to do with the film [called *Innocence of Muslims*]. It was a planned attack, not a protest." Senator Lindsey Graham, speaking on October 14 on CBS's *Face the Nation*, had declared that the intelligence community in Libya knew from the start that the consulate had been the object of a terrorist attack, a comment that was corroborated by the CIA station chief in Libya.

The September 12 DIA note we cited a few lines above had been handed to Hillary Clinton, the Secretary of Defense Leon Panetta, the Joint Chiefs of Staff, and the National Security Council. It mentioned that a certain Abdul Baset [AZUZ], the leader of the Brigades of the Imprisoned Sheikh Omar Abdel Rahman, had been sent over by Al-Qaeda's Ayman al-Zawahiri to lay the foundations for the organization in Libya. The main objective was as much to join other groups in overthrowing Gaddafi as to wage a war against the Americans. But despite all this evidence, the Sunday following the Benghazi assault (September 16), the American Ambassador to the United Nations, Susan Rice, did not say a word on the famous DIA's note while featuring on several talk shows on American TV networks, as she did not reveal anything about a planned attack: "Putting together the best information that we have available to us today, our current assessment is that what happened in Benghazi was in fact initially a spontaneous reaction to what had just transpired hours before in Cairo", she said emphatically, speaking of the protests that had taken place in the Egyptian capital in response to the video *Innocence of Muslims*. Why did Rice take such a stance? Because the office of the Director of National Intelligence (DNI) had removed specific references to Al-Qaeda and terrorism from the unclassified talking points given to the American Ambassador, apparently with the agreement of the CIA and the FBI, as reported by *CBS News*. The day after Rice appeared on American TV shows, *Fox News* reported that a source had stated that no demonstration had taken place in front of the American consulate in Benghazi before the attack, so that the latter was not the result of a gathering gone wrong. On September 21, a few American officials had finally been forthright when they had claimed that the "heavily armed" extremists who had laid siege to the consulate had used "military-style tactics" in what seemed to be a "sophisticated operation." On September 28, it was the turn of Shawn Turner, the Director of Public Affairs for the Director of National Intelligence, to refute the State Department's assumption. Turner even alluded to Al-Qaeda: "As we learned more about the attack, we revised our initial assessment to reflect new information indicating that it was a deliberate and organized terrorist attack carried out by extremists", he said in a statement. "It remains unclear if any group or person exercised overall command and control of the attack, and if extremist group leaders directed their members to participate. However, we do assess that some of those involved were linked to groups affiliated with, or sympathetic to Al-Qaeda." On November 2, the case was back in the media when *Fox News* reported that the U.S. military intelligence had notified senior commanders, only four hours after the attack began, that the Al-Qaeda-affiliated group Ansar al-Sharia had led the insurrection. This proves that the State Department not only withheld information but lied to the American public from the outset. The U.S. Benghazi mission, as we pointed out before, had called for an emergency meeting in August 2012 due to the strong presence of Al-Qaeda in the area. Let's remember that in a cable marked "secret", the local State Department's Regional Security Officer (RSO) had expressed his doubts about the protection of the consulate in the event of an attack. This officer, we must repeat it, had been informed of the presence of a dozen Islamist militias and Al-Qaeda training camps in the region. So, why hiding those facts to the public?

The assailants of the diplomatic mission belonged to a collection of organizations that operated under the leadership of Ansar al-Sharia, a sort of subcontractor for Al-Qaeda. As a matter of fact, a few of those assailants were directly linked to the latter terrorist group. These were an Egyptian trained in Afghan camps at the end of the 1980s; a man close to Ayman al-Zawahiri, whom he had met in the months preceding the attack; a former Libyan bodyguard of Osama bin Laden, as well as one of his former drivers; and a former Al-Qaeda courier. The former Libyan bodyguard of Osama bin Laden was one Faraj al-Chalabi, who fled Libya to settle in Pakistan shortly after the Benghazi operation. Suspected of having delivered equipment to the insurgents, Chalabi was arrested and returned to Libya, where he was interrogated and mysteriously released. Among all those gangsters, though, there is one man that is of particular interest to us: Abu Sufian Ibrahim Ahmed Hamouda bin Qumu, a former Guantanamo detainee who is said to have acted as a trainer for the jihadists in Benghazi. Qumu was part of the first version of "Afghan Arabs" fighters who went to Afghanistan back in the 80s to help the mujahideen in their war against the Soviets. When Osama bin Laden had moved to Sudan, Qumu had followed him, as he did later when the former Al-Qaeda leader was expelled from that country. Qumu was finally arrested in Pakistan after the September 11, 2001, attacks and transferred to the U.S. detention center at Guantanamo Bay, where he spent six years. All information regarding the links between Qumu and Al-Qaeda had been recorded in a directory used to determine the level of threat posed by the detainees at the Guantanamo prison. This directory, called the *JTF-GTMO Matrix of Threat Indicators for Enemy Combatants*, labeled Qumu as an "associate" of Osama bin Laden. His name was also found on the laptop of an Al-Qaeda agent by the name of Mustafa Al-Hawsawi, one of the group's many financial facilitators before the September 11, 2001, attacks. Qumu was transferred from Guantanamo to Libya on September 28, 2007, and released in 2010 as part of an agreement between the United States and the Gaddafi regime. He then became the leader of Ansar al-Sharia in Derna, Libya. The jihadist denied all those facts, but a report published in August 2012 by the Library of Congress, together with the Defense Department, had even gone so far as to describe him as "the new face of Al-Qaeda in Libya." Qumu and his Ansar al-Sharia fighters were "believed to be close to the Al-Qaeda clandestine network" in Libya, a network headed by members who received orders directly from the organization's top management in Pakistan. Sources say that Qumu's men were in Benghazi before the September 11, 2012, attack, but it is unknown if they were there to prepare for the assault. An intriguing fact remains: Ambassador Christopher Stevens, along with other State Department diplomats, had worked hard to ensure that the former Guantanamo detainees who had been transferred to Gaddafi prisons were treated well. Another "illustrious" terrorist, Mokhtar Belmokhtar, a long-time commander of Al-Qaeda in the Islamic Maghreb, reportedly received a call from a member of Ansar al-Sharia congratulating him on the night of the attack on Benghazi, which suggests that the assault was really an order from Al-Qaeda, possibly from its leader Ayman al-Zawahiri himself.

Clinton's Jihadists

We must devote a few more lines to the Benghazi fiasco since so many blunders were committed in this affair that it would take an entire book to make a full account of it. On the evening of the assault on the consulate, three members of the February 17th Martyrs Brigade, hired by the State Department as a quick reaction force to protect the diplomatic corps, were present alongside five armed security officers, a couple of Libyan national police officers and five unarmed members of Blue Mountain Group, a security firm. In short, a very light company, considering that it had to fight against up to sixty men, some of them carrying grenade launchers. The State Department faced a barrage of criticism in this regard, especially because of the militia it had picked for the "quick reaction force", the February 17th Martyrs Brigade. For a start, the name conjures up anger, hostility, and suggests that we are truly dealing with a radical Islamist organization. According to reports, during the night of the attack against the consulate, the three members of the brigade refused to fire on the insurgents, preferring instead to negotiate. Did they act this way for a purely logical reason? Let's state it clearly: hiring this militia was a risky and unwise decision as it became known afterwards that several of its members never made a secret of their sympathy for Al-Qaeda. A sympathy that was highly noticeable on its Facebook page where we could see the Al-Qaeda flag and a photograph related to the latter's Syrian branch, the Al-Nusra Front, as well as several texts glorifying the Ansar al-Sharia group. No wonder the February 17th Martyrs Brigade was run in part by Abdelhakim Belhaj, the former Libyan Islamic Fighting Group's military commander, who was thoroughly explored in a previous section. As a reversal of fortune, the militia was sanctioned by the UN Security Council and placed on the U.S.'s and U.K.'s list of terrorist entities. Sources revealed to *The Daily Beast* that American intelligence had intercepted a telephone conversation in which a Libyan politician who supported Al-Qaeda and a member of the brigade were talking about demobilizing the latter on the night of the attack against the consulate. Like Ansar al-Sharia, the February 17th Martyrs Brigade is part of the Shura Council of Benghazi Revolutionaries, largely infiltrated by Islamists. Reports from the Republican wing of the U.S. House of Representatives concluded that the militia also participated in the kidnapping of American citizens, among other crimes. So, why did the State Department choose that organization to protect the consulate? This question has unfortunately remained unanswered.

Within hours of the assault, the United States dispatched a "security team" whose task was to evacuate the consulate staff. Strangely, this team did not come from Benghazi, but Tripoli, the Libyan capital, the reason being that the Americans had no decent strike force on-site, in a city at war. That "security team" from Tripoli was airlifted to Benghazi, but due to the chaos the city was plunged into, the Libyan government had managed to find another militia, the Libya Shield Force, to provide transportation and an armed escort from the airport. Let's take a moment to talk about the Libya Shield Force, as we have done for the February 17th Martyrs Brigade. Here again, we are dealing with an organization that follows in the footsteps of Al-Qaeda. This is precisely what the U.S. government said loud and clear in a special report published in August 2012—just a month before the assault on Benghazi—by the Library of Congress and the United States Federal Research Division, under an agreement with the Combating Terrorism Technical Support Office. The Libya Shield Force was formed in 2012 by Libya's Ministry of Defense, but was soon designated as a terrorist entity by the Libyan Parliament. One wonders, therefore, who in the national government could have chosen that organization to provide assistance to the American "security team" that had been dispatched to rescue the consulate staff. In those days, the Libya Shield Force was divided into three branches: first, the Libya Shield 1, a member, like the February 17th Martyrs Brigade, of the Shura Council of Benghazi Revolutionaries; second, the Western Shield, involved in fighting on the outskirts of Tripoli and headed by a man close to Al-Qaeda, Abd al-Muhsin al-Libi, also known as Ibrahim Ali Abu Bakr or Ibrahim Tantoush; third, the Central Shield, serving the General National Congress. These three factions had been designated as terrorist entities by the Libyan House of Representatives. Ibrahim Tantoush is certainly the leader who has stood out the most within the Libya Shield Force. In the summer of 2012, the American Green Berets had set out to fix up a military base located 16 miles west of Tripoli to train the first anti-terrorist fighters who were to join the new Libyan Army. Less than two years later, the base came under the control of Tantoush's Western Shield. Things began to deteriorate in June 2013 when two rival militias, including the Western Shield, stormed the training center. According to two U.S. officials who spoke to *The Daily Beast* on condition of anonymity, no member of the U.S. forces was working on the base at the time, which allowed the militias to seize all the weapons that had been stored there, including M-4 rifles, pistols, military vehicles, and ammunition. It is worth noting that in 2000, Ibrahim Tantoush had been charged by the Southern District of New York with having participated in the planning of the 1998 attacks against the American Embassies in Kenya and Tanzania.

Was the Benghazi Consulate the Nerve Center of Arms Sale in Libya?

Many raised questions about the presence of the consulate in Benghazi and its real purpose. Officially, Ambassador J. Christopher Stevens served as a liaison between the Obama administration and the Libyan opposition. But did he hide another reality? While we are at it, let's write a few lines about J. Christopher Stevens, an "idealist" fond of Benghazi, as he was portrayed in *GQ* magazine. During the 2011 revolution, he spent most of his time roaming around the streets to explore every corner of the city and blend in with the local population. Upon his arrival on Libyan soil, Stevens held multiple meetings with rebel leaders, which enabled him to glean information on the state of affairs: who does what, when, where, and how. We can surely say that behind Hillary Clinton's decisions on the Libyan question lurked, at some point, Stevens's influence. But was this romantic liberal a hawk deep within himself? Good question. *The New York Times* reported in December 2012 that the ex-ambassador had backed a request for an arms sales permit that a trafficker named Marc Turi had filed with the State Department. According to the *Times*, Turi's first request was denied in March 2011, but a second one was approved in May after the trafficker said that he intended to ship his weapons not to Libya but Qatar, a United States ally. This strategy was not enough to render the whole operation legal because two months later, agents from the Homeland Security Department and the Defense Department "stormed his Scottsdale residence with a search warrant, seizing evidence of criminal conduct." It is somewhat surprising that the State

Department trusted Turi, a man whose criminal record dates back to 1986 when he was arrested for fraud and credit card forgery. A year later, as a sophomore at Arizona State University, he walked off with $10,000 worth of computer equipment. Within months, according to the *NYT*, "he was a convicted felon, stripped of civil rights and barred from possessing firearms." He later moved to Los Angeles, "went absent without leave, returned to Arizona, stole a car and ripped off some checks." In 2005, he began selling ammunition and weapons through Turi Defense Group LLC. In 2010, the value of the contracts signed between this company and the United States government stood at $14 million. Turi was teaming up at the time with a subcontractor, Arlo Dolarian, who was under federal investigation for possible human rights violations. Then came the Arab Spring. A week before J. Christopher Stevens was sworn in as Ambassador to Libya, Turi exchanged emails with him, seeking help for his State Department permit. But as we have seen, the Homeland Security Department and the Defense Department agents raided his residence weeks later. As a result, the arms transfer never took place. In 2014, Turi was finally "accused of lying to the State Department and violating U.S. arms-export laws", even though no shipment was ever delivered by the trafficker to Libya or Qatar.

Was Turi's operation the only time Stevens served as a go-between in the delivery of weapons to the rebels? Perhaps not. According to *Business Insider*, in March 2011, the ex-diplomat had established a channel with Abdelhakim Belhaj, the famous Libyan Islamic Fighting Group's military commander. Belhaj is said to have organized, among other things, the delivery of a 400-ton weapons shipment to the Syrian rebels. Another media, the *Wall Street Journal (WSJ)*, revealed that the CIA had used the consulate as a base of operations for the same reasons. That would make sense since diplomatic representations have always been anchor points of intelligence services, regardless of the country. But the Benghazi Consulate had pushed the logic to an extreme: according to the *WSJ*, of the 30 American officials evacuated from Benghazi after the attack, only seven worked for the State Department; the others belonged mainly to the CIA. The agency's prime objective in Benghazi was to monitor jihadist groups such as Ansar al-Sharia and Al-Qaeda in the Islamic Maghreb, but according to several unnamed sources, the diplomatic mission and its annex were also used to conceal weapons belonging to the former Libyan regime in order to transfer them to anti-Assad rebels in Syria. At first glance, this assumption seems far-fetched, but it is not. When the U.S. Senate Intelligence Committee released its investigation report into the Benghazi events, a section had remained classified. It was later discovered that the section in question referred to a secret agreement reached in early 2012 between Turkey and the United States, whereby Turkey, along with Saudi Arabia and Qatar, was to provide funds for the establishment of an arms transport network called the "rat line." In this maneuver, the CIA, with the support of the British MI6, was responsible for getting arms from Gaddafi's arsenals to send them to Syria. For that purpose, front companies were set up and retired U.S. soldiers hired to manage procurement and shipping. The entire operation was conducted from the office of the CIA director David Petraeus. After the September 11, 2012, attack, the intelligence agency dropped out of the operation, but the "rat line" remained active. With or without the CIA, though, the main operatives behind this "rat line" quickly lost control of the weapons delivery. Portable surface-to-air missiles (MANPAD), for instance, were resold to jihadist groups such as the Al-Nusra Front and the Islamic State. On November 27, 2012, for that matter, one of these groups shot down a Syrian Army helicopter, using a MANPAD. In June 2012, *The New York Times* reported that CIA officers were secretly operating in southern Turkey to help their allies choose the Syrian opposition groups that were to receive weapons, including automatic rifles, unguided rocket-propelled grenade launchers (RPGs), ammunition and anti-tank weapons. Everything was shipped across the Turkish border through a network of intermediaries, including the Muslim Brotherhood, with which the Obama administration had resumed discussions. The Americans paid a heavy price for that association because the same Muslim Brotherhood was not as selective as the CIA when it came to distributing the weapons.

Now, was the Benghazi Consulate really acting as a cover for arms trafficking? Ambassador Stevens's diary, found in the ruins of the building, showed that on September 10 he had met the chief operating officer of the CIA team settled in the annex located not far from the consulate. The next day, the last of his existence, Stevens had this time held a meeting with a representative of the charter company Al-Marfa Shipping and Maritime Services, which was overseeing the smooth running of weapons shipments. There is no evidence here that the former ambassador turned out to be the mastermind of arms trafficking to the Syrian rebels, but it is clear that he did not content himself with playing second fiddle. Most of all, the whole process had to be kept secret. The CIA officers involved in the agency's missions in Libya had to undergo frequent polygraph tests, the purpose of which was to verify whether any of them had spoken to the media. An unusual process, even for an intelligence service. "Agency employees are generally subject to the polygraph every three or four years", said Robert Baer, a former CIA case officer, on the matter. It was necessary to hide, from these curious media, that the United States, Qatar and Turkey were violating the embargo on the sale of weapons to Libya imposed by the UN resolution 1970. An old tactic the Americans have used many times. But this was, above all, a snub inflicted on the United States Congress, as all CIA's covert operation must be explained in great detail in a document submitted to the leaders of that institution for approval. But nothing has been done in this regard in the Libyan case. A panel of UN experts, to give an example, reported that 55 containers carrying 1,103 tons of ammunition were discovered by Greek authorities in 2013 on board the ship Nour-M; 1,103 tons, nothing less. The freighter was flying the flag of Turkey and the shipment seized was to be sent to Libya. The same panel of experts had received information on an Airbus A320, operated by the Afriqiyah Airways airline, which had flown from Istanbul to Tripoli with weapons on board, all intended for a country facing a merciless war: Syria.

THE DARK SIDE OF SYRIA'S WAR

Syria is the third and last stage of our journey in the Middle East. This country, which has been at war for the last decade, has not escaped intrigues and backroom deals that Iraq and Libya had experienced before. And here again, the players that lined up to put on a "sound and light" show in Libya featuring rebels dipped into fundamentalism were back for an encore in Syria. These players, needless to say, are the United States, the United Kingdom and France, supported by the same allies they had worked with in Libya: Turkey, Saudi Arabia, and Qatar. This "sound and light" show was especially distressing, if not pitiful, and its first signs did not appear during the Arab Spring but years earlier when, in Washington, talks about reshaping the Middle East were going on. Syria's main flaw was that it was—and still is—Iran's ally, the U.S.'s sworn enemy. It was therefore necessary to weaken the Syrian edifice in order to bring about the collapse of the Syria-Iran alliance. But since Iran has a much more significant military program than Syria's, it was then easier for Washington to go after the less powerful of the two states. In 2011, if the Oval Office had been occupied by Georges W. Bush rather than Barack Obama, the United States would have likely intervened directly in Syria against the government of Bashar al-Assad. Washington actually did intervene, but not against al-Assad because as fate would have it, American soldiers strolled alongside those of Hezbollah and Iran against ISIS troops. That was a strange combination of circumstances: to defeat fanatics, the United States had to team up with other fanatics. This whim of geopolitics makes one think of drug trafficking: in order to catch major traffickers, authorities do not hesitate to call on street-level dealers. But this strategy is highly questionable because drug trafficking has never been so lucrative. And this is why Syria's conflict has produced no concrete results so far, apart from the fact that the Syrian soil is on the way to becoming the tomb of the Islamic State. But the snake will not die until its head is cut off, and everyone in Western chancelleries knows where this head is to be found: in Saudi Arabia, Qatar, and Pakistan. But this is a whole different story.

In both Syria and Libya, the shadow of the State Department has hung over the conflict, and if it had not been for President Obama, the United States would have fought along ISIS and Al-Qaeda, an initiative that would have been hardly defendable, but which seemed, to a certain extent, purely logical among their liberal allies in Europe. The delusion of grandeur, though, did not please a majority of French and British parliamentarians who rejected the idea of direct intervention advocated by their government, while in the United States, the soon-to-be lame duck President was able to curb the enthusiasm of the hawks at the State Department who did not care that Syria had been stormed by Islamists. Those had wanted Gaddafi's head to be offered on a silver platter, and once that request was granted, it was the turn of al-Assad. But the President-dictator is still in power, ten years and hundreds of thousands of deaths later.

The Number One Priority: Destabilizing Syria

In March 2007, the renowned journalist Seymour Hersh published an 8,000-word article in *The New Yorker* wherein he argued that the American government was getting ready to embark on a major shift in its foreign policy in the Middle East. Titled *The Redirection*, the article suggested that the Bush administration had tilted its support away from the Shiite community in Iraq in order to give it to various Sunni groups around the Middle East. This new approach was to help bring about a regime change in Syria and lead to a possible attack on Iran. Let's recall that the same year, the retired general and former Supreme Allied Commander of NATO in Europe, Wesley Clark, had said in an interview he had given to Amy Goodman of *Democracy Now!* that a colleague of his, a general of the U.S. Joint Chiefs of Staff, had confessed to him that the Bush administration, in the aftermath of 9/11, was planning to attack seven countries, namely Iraq, Syria, Lebanon, Libya, Somalia, Sudan and Iran, over five years. That program was probably deemed too ambitious to be taken seriously by the general staff, but it was nevertheless part of a logic formulated in the *Project for the New American Century* (PNAC), as we have seen in the section on the intervention in Iraq. The "hawkish" wing of the Bush administration thus called for an overhaul of the U.S. policy in the Middle East that would start in Iraq and subsequently spread out to Iran, Syria, and perhaps even Lebanon, which was publicly confirmed by the ex-National Security Advisor and ex-Secretary of State, Condoleeza Rice. With a disturbing simplicity, Ms. Rice had explained to the Senate Committee on Foreign Relations that her government had opted for "a new strategic alignment in the Middle East" in conjunction with Sunni "reformists"—that is, the "moderates," according to the language strongly promoted at the time by the tenants of the White House—against the Shiites who were "on the other side of that divide." Rice and her mates in Washington seemed to have forgotten, though, that the main terrorist groups—the PLO in the 70s and 80s, Al-Qaeda, the Islamic State, Hamas, and the Taliban—are part of the Sunni movement and are backed up by equally Sunni countries. No doubt the members of the Bush administration demonstrated a naïve and harmful optimism by placing the Salafist Islamists on the side of the moderates. That said, they had nonetheless succeeded in imposing their guideline, and the influential Rand Corporation, a few years later, followed suit with a strategy worthy of Machiavelli by suggesting that the U.S. government implement a "divide and conquer" policy, arguing that the new Obama administration needed to take advantage of the Sunni-Shiite rift to team up with the radical Sunnis. Condoleeza Rice was quite knowledgeable about the new strategic alignment (or *The Redirection*) she had referred to, since it had been shaped in part by one of her close associates, Deputy National Security Advisor Elliott Abrams, with the active support of Vice President Dick Cheney, the former American Ambassador to Iraq, Zalmay Khalilzad, and, above all, Saudi Prince Bandar bin Sultan, a friend of President Bush. Nobody was taken aback when Bandar got involved in the project; the prince just could not resist the temptation of multiplying acts aimed at putting his country at the center stage in order to make it the official leader of the Middle East and, why not, of the Muslim world. The Bush government, by accepting that Bandar becomes a strategist in *The Redirection*, showed that it had no qualms about collaborating with those famous "radical Sunnis." The history of the former Saudi Ambassador to Washington is evidence of a very questionable ideological position. Let's see the outline of this position to better understand this shady character's record.

To do this, we must first return to the events surrounding the terrorist attacks on September 11, 2001, to look into the case of two of the hijackers, Nawaf al-Hazmi and Khalid al-Mihdhar. When, on January 15, 2000, these two men landed at Los Angeles International Airport on a flight from Kuala Lumpur, Malaysia, they were greeted by one Omar al-Bayoumi, a Saudi national who drove them to San Diego after inviting them to stay in his apartment, at least until they find another one, which they were quick to do. Al-Bayoumi was a real benefactor for the two hijackers. Among other services, he helped them pay the rent in addition to lending them his cell phone, finding a translator and obtaining documents such as a driver's license as well as a social security card. Most of all, he provided them with information on some flight training schools in the area. For 35 years, Omar al-Bayoumi lived a peaceful life in his native Saudi Arabia, where he worked for a time for the Saudi Ministry of Defense and Aviation. But in August 1994, he decided to move out to the United States and settle in San Diego. Four years later, an anonymous contributor raised $550,000 to build a mosque in San Diego and demanded that al-Bayoumi be hired as a maintenance manager. There is no evidence that the latter held this job, but one thing is certain: he was, at some point, a "ghost" employee of Ercan, a subsidiary of a contractor linked to the Saudi Civil Aviation

Administration. A "ghost" employee because the man had the habit of never showing up for work, a flaw that did not prevent him from receiving a salary of $2,800 per month, increased, curiously, to $3,700 sometime after al-Hazmi and al-Mihdhar arrived in the United States. Al-Bayoumi was often equipped with a video camera during his travels, which earned him to be suspected of spying for the Saudi government. Especially that between January and May 2000, he made a hundred calls to establishments belonging to the Saudi state. One of his main points of contact was the Saudi Embassy in Washington, whose person in charge was none other than Prince Bandar. Al-Bayoumi has nevertheless always claimed that he unintentionally met the two hijackers in a Los Angeles restaurant, not at the airport. And the FBI went further by concluding that the Saudi was not guilty of anything, that he was not a spy and that the two hijackers had no accomplice in San Diego. That was a curious conclusion since al-Bayoumi had several disreputable friends, one of whom is of great interest: Osama Basnan. Basnan appeared on the FBI's radar as early as 1992 when he was affiliated to the Islamic Jihad in Eritrea, which was said to be close to Al-Qaeda. On October 17, 1992, while living in Washington, Basnan hosted a party for Omar Abdel Rahman, the spiritual leader who served a life sentence—until his death in February 2017—for his involvement in the first terrorist attacks on the World Trade Center in 1993. Thanks to a case the FBI had built on Basnan, we know that, just like Omar al-Bayoumi, he worked for the Saudi government despite his links with radical Islamists. And according to the Congress's Joint Inquiry report on 9/11, he was also employed by the Saudi Arabian Education Mission at the Embassy in Washington. In the months preceding the terrorist attacks in September 2001, Basnan's wife, Majeda Dweikat, was receiving between $2,000 and $3,500 a month (sources differ) from Princess Haifa bint Faisal, the wife of the illustrious Prince Bandar. It was Basnan himself who had asked for help from the Embassy on behalf of his wife who was supposedly sick. Those payments were sent to the Basnans until May 2002. Some sources say the couple received, in all, $51,000, but others reported that the figures were $74,000. On at least one occasion, Basnan is said to have been given $15,000 directly from an account belonging to Prince Bandar. Princess Haifa was apparently furious about having been tricked and stated that she was unaware the funds had been misappropriated. It was through Washington's Riggs Bank, Prince Bandar's favorite financial institution, that the Princess's money was sent to the Basnan-Dweikat couple. For that matter, in the aftermath of 9/11, the Saudi Ambassador's accounts were investigated by the FBI. No surprise, the Bureau had found nothing suspicious. Yet, on July 10, 2001, the Saudi Embassy in Washington had sent a check for $70,000 to two Saudis in Massachusetts, one of whom had sent, the same day, a check for $20,000 to a third Saudi who was living at the same address as Aafia Siddiqui, a Pakistani microbiologist linked to Al-Qaeda and found guilty of attempting to kill American soldiers in Afghanistan. In light of what we know, either Bandar and his princess were easy to fool, or they were mixed up in dubious ventures. Osama Basnan was finally deported to Saudi Arabia in August 2002, but he would feature in one last episode of this bewildering saga on April 24 and 25, 2002. At that time, Prince Abdullah, then-King of Saudi Arabia, was in Texas for a meeting with President Bush. The FBI had been informed that three of the men who appeared on its watch list were among Abdullah's entourage on that trip. The Bureau was ready to catch them, but the State Department turned down its request. Again, no surprise here, but a man we know had one for us: Osama Basnan, who was in Houston at the very same time for a "business trip." The event had been pointed out by the congressional committee investigating 9/11, but no conclusion had been drawn from it, other than Basnan had possibly met a Saudi government official who could have given him money. How much and why? Nothing has been revealed about this.

There was another shady character in the Saudi community, a man by the name of Fahad al-Thumairy, a former diplomat who served as a liaison between the Saudi consulate in Los Angeles and the King Fahd mosque in Culver City, California. Like Omar al-Bayoumi, al-Thumairy had met the two hijackers in the objective, it seemed, of helping them settle on Californian soil. Details of al-Bayoumi's telephone calls showed that the latter called al-Thumairy several times between December 1998 and December 2000. No information was disclosed on the content of these calls, but this adds a layer of strangeness to the atmosphere that surrounded those controversial figures. A strange atmosphere that nine members of the 9/11 Commission staff could not clear up when they interviewed Basnan, al-Thumairy and al-Bayoumi in Saudi Arabia in 2003 and 2004. Al-Thumairy, in two interviews, made contradictory comments and denied knowing al-Bayoumi, Khalid al-Mihdhar and Nawaf al-Hazmi. It was only after an official who accompanied him whispered a few words in his ear that he admitted to having heard of al-Bayoumi in the news. When one of the investigators told him that witnesses had testified to seeing him with al-Bayoumi, al-Thumairy took a break before retorting that those witnesses had surely mistaken him for someone else. When finally told about al-Bayoumi's calls to his home, the man looked puzzled. Perhaps, he replied, someone other than al-Bayoumi had used his phone? The latter made a more favorable impression and repeated what he had already said, that his meeting with the hijackers had been purely coincidental and that he had decided not to pursue his relationship with them. As for Basnan, the commissioner who interviewed him, Dietrich Snell, said that he lacked credibility, that he provided vague answers and, as al-Thumairy, that he made contradictory comments. None of the three men had to suffer the yoke of American or Saudi justice.

We can tell a few more "anecdotes" about Prince Bandar. Like this one, for instance, which involves the phone number of an obscure organization found in the notebook of Abu Zubaydah, one of Al-Qaeda's former leaders jailed in the United States. The organization is called ASPCOL, as in "Aspen" and "Colorado." What was so unusual about ASPCOL? A thorny problem: the FBI had discovered that this company was an umbrella in charge of the maintenance of Prince Bandar's residence in Aspen. But because the subject had likely been deemed far too sensitive by the Bureau, the investigation had not gone any further. We have never known why ASPCOL's number wound up in the phone book of one of the actors of 9/11, any more than we have learned why the phone number of one of the Saudi Embassy guards in Washington was also found in the same phone book. There is one final number, this one belonging to an individual whose name has not been released and that was found in an Al-Qaeda's "safe house" in Pakistan. The individual said that he did not know why his number landed in that safe house, but he made a surprising revelation: he used to provide services to a couple of Saudis who worked as Bandar's assistants. One last thing in relation to the former Saudi Ambassador to Washington that one cannot fail to mention. It concerns an incident involving two more Saudis, Mohammed al-Qudhacein and Hamdan al-Shalawi, aboard an America West Airlines aircraft in 1999. These two men had exhibited a strange behavior during the flight and asked questions that had aroused the suspicion of the flight attendants. Worse: al-Qudhacein made two attempts to enter the cockpit, which resulted in the emergency landing of the aircraft. The FBI had investigated the case, but without ever accusing the two Saudis. It was once again an odd decision as it was known that the two men's plane tickets had been paid for by the Saudi Embassy in Washington. One wonders if Prince Bandar and the Embassy staff knew that al-Shalawi had spent some time in Al-Qaeda camps in Afghanistan where he had received training in explosives. The 9/11 congressional committee had touched on the matter, but once more, the two suspects avoided being brought to justice.

We can clearly see, with these typical cases, that for Washington, associating with die-hard obscurantists is a recurring ritual. In Syria, the United States, as in the past in Afghanistan, has based its hopes on individuals and groups that gravitate around the Islamist orbit and maintain close relations with Saudi Arabia, a country that is proud to spread its Wahhabi ideology all over the world. But the Saudis were not the only ones involved in a mess that gives off foul smells. As part of its new *Redirection* policy, the Bush administration had offered a billion dollars to the government of Fouad Siniora in Lebanon, even though the latter had allowed funds to end up in the hands of radical Sunni groups. Other governments, same procedures. *The Redirection*, in fact, was only the extension of a policy of destabilization that started well before 2007 and that primarily targeted Syria, even if the Syrian government had been very useful to the United States in the aftermath of 9/11. This was the time when the Syrian secret services had provided the Americans with internal files relating to the activities of the Muslim Brotherhood in Syria and Germany. Even better: the same secret services had foiled an Al-Qaeda attack on the command post of the U.S. Navy's 5th Fleet in Bahrain. The CIA, on its side, had found a good partner in Damascus, where it could rely on its counterpart to extract valuable information from Al-Qaeda members thanks to "enhanced interrogation techniques." But the honeymoon could not last: when Washington realized that Syria was allowing rebels to slip across Iraq to join the insurgents against American forces, everyone knew, from then on, that the circumstantial alliance had just been broken off. This was in 2003; the Syrian services had arranged for the transfer of thousands of combatants from Libya, Saudi Arabia and Tunisia into the Iraqi territory to unleash hell on the American troops in response to the sanctions imposed by the United States on Syria for its alleged links to terrorism. After all, hadn't Paul Wolfowitz, the Deputy Secretary of Defense, declared, a month after the invasion of Iraq, that there needed to be a regime change in Syria? The diplomatic relations between the two countries deteriorated mainly from 2006, the year Washington began funding a London-based group of Syrian exiles called the *Movement for Justice and Development*, whose main sponsor was the Muslim Brotherhood. The *Movement for Justice and Development*'s "public relations manager" was a man in the name of Ausama Monajed, one of the most important spokesmen of the Syrian National Council, a structure itself largely controlled by the Muslim Brotherhood. No less than $6 million was donated to the *Movement for Justice and Development*, which owned, among other things, a television station called *Barada-TV* that broadcast its programming in Syria. It was around this time that Vice President Dick Cheney, accompanied by Prince Bandar bin Sultan, paid a visit to Prince Abdullah of Saudi Arabia to talk about the destabilization campaign against the Shiites. In the months following that visit, the United States attempted to weaken the Hezbollah with funds that came from Saudi coffers. Washington had just gotten into *The Redirection* with full force, and it was not long before the petrodollars were poured into Syria for the same reasons they had been poured into Siniora's Lebanon. No luck for al-Assad, in August 2007, the Israeli air force put an end to its nuclear ambitions by bombing a reactor in the city of Deir ez-Zor. A year later, almost to the day, two snipers from the 13ᵗʰ flotilla (Shayetet 13) of the Israeli Navy killed one of the Syrian nuclear program officials, General Mohammed Suleiman, in Tartus. With these two blows, the Israeli government had issued a warning to the Syrian government by showing that its patience had come to the breaking point. Confused, al-Assad later tried to reach a peace agreement with his Israeli neighbor, but the Bush administration firmly opposed it and made it clearly known to Tel-Aviv. The same administration, on October 26, 2008, ordered the CIA to carry out an attack near the Syrian city of Al-Bukamal, which attack targeted the network of Al-Qaeda-linked foreign fighters moving freely through Syria to cross the Iraqi border. One Al-Qaeda asset, Abu Ghadiya, was killed in the operation. As a response, Syria closed two American institutions in Damascus: a school called the Damascus Community School, and a cultural center.

The British ally, it seemed, did not wish to be cast aside in *The Redirection*. During a debate on French television, a former French Foreign Minister, Roland Dumas, gave a good overview of the United Kingdom's plans to destabilize Syria: "I am going to tell you something. I was in England two years before the hostilities began in Syria. I was there by chance for […] business, not at all for Syria. I met with British officials, some of whom are friends of mine, and they confessed […] that they were preparing something in Syria. This was in Britain, not America. Britain was preparing the invasion of rebels into Syria […]. I just need to say that this operation goes way back. It was prepared, conceived and planned." If Dumas told the truth, this means that the British government had planned an intervention for 2009, two years before the Arab Spring. Was this project serious? One thing is sure, in 2011, London was ready to carry the torch of the anti-Assad rebellion. Leaked emails from the private intelligence firm Stratfor confirmed that during the Arab Spring, the training of the Syrian opposition forces by the American and British armies was well underway. The clearly stated objective of the United States and the United Kingdom was, from the outset, to bring about the collapse of Bashar al-Assad, whether this had to be done from within or outside the regime. Meanwhile, CIA officers, along with Israeli and Jordanian commandos, were training rebels of the Free Syrian Army on the Jordanian-Syrian border.

The Truth About the First Days of the Conflict

The Western world and its media networks remained rather silent as strong opposition to the Iranian government took to the streets in late 2017 and early 2018. Few officials in Western chancelleries called for the Iranian government to put a stop to the crackdown that left a little more than fifteen dead among the demonstrators. Perhaps these chancelleries had in mind the Vienna Agreement on the Iranian nuclear program that they wanted to preserve. See the contrast between that relative silence about Iran and the situation that prevailed in spring 2011 when the same chancelleries had voiced their concern at the start of the uprisings in Libya and Syria. While senators Joe Lieberman, John McCain and Lindsey Graham publicly pressed for a regime change in Syria, at the White House, Hillary Clinton followed their lead, deploring the number of dead civilians during the Arab Spring demonstrations. The Secretary of State maintained this rhetoric throughout 2011, being careful not to recall an important fact: in the first 10 to 12 months of the conflict, out of approximately 5,000 people who died during the protests, 478 were police officers and 2,091 were part of the military or the security forces. All victims, the protesters?

The story began in Daraa, in the south of Syria, with a simple graffiti: "It's your turn, doctor", had written a young boy, referring to Bashar al-Assad, a career ophthalmologist. Arrested by the Syrian police, the youth was reportedly beaten, which gave thousands of Syrians a good excuse to gather in the streets of Daraa and clash with the government forces. On March 15, 2011, demonstrators in Damascus, the capital, called out for major political reforms and the release of numerous prisoners. In an attempt to ease tensions, the government offered to release the graffiti artist and his companions, a move that was not enough to cool things down. A few days after the protests kicked off, seven police officers were killed and the Baath Party headquarters destroyed by demonstrators armed to the teeth. In early April, another group of armed men ambushed Syrian soldiers, killing about two dozen of them. The rest of the story varied from day to day: either President al-Assad chose to maintain the hard line and persisted in suppressing the demonstrations, or he opted for an open policy by sending emissaries to the opponents. The Syrian dictator, who surely wanted to save time and project a good image of himself, ousted a governor and a general responsible for the bloody repression, an approach that came with an announcement on major reforms: formation of a new government, lifting of the state of emergency, abolition of the Supreme Court of State Security, proposals for a general amnesty, and new rules on the right of citizens to participate in peaceful demonstrations. Whether this "openness" was only a smokescreen or a real desire to grant more political space to the Syrian population, the demonstrations nevertheless continued at an accelerated pace. During this episode of Syria's tumultuous political life, the observers in search of information could only refer to Western politicians and the mainstream media, which painted a one-sided picture of the situation. For these politicians and media, only the regime was to blame for the chaos that reigned in the streets of major Syrian cities. The massacres perpetrated against the Syrian military and security forces were concealed from the Western public so as not to harm the official narrative. Yet, if the demonstrators showed all the spontaneity usually seen in such opposition movements, some of them rather resorted to organized violence that seemed to be evidence of a manipulation performed by foreign groups or countries. Strangely, *CNN* played fair on August 2, 2011, during a TV report about a video shared on the Web in which rebels were seen dumping the bodies of Syrian soldiers over a bridge parapet. That day, we all learned from *CNN*, which, until then, had accustomed us to selective information confirming the positions of the Obama clan, that the video was not about a fake news story. In October 2011, pro-Assad demonstrations took place in Aleppo and in Damascus, where tens and even hundreds of thousands of people took to the streets not to demand the resignation of their president, but to support him. Once again, it was radio silence in the Western liberal media, a silence that no one wanted to break, except to suggest that the said demonstrations had been staged by the regime. One wonders if al-Assad was as unpopular as the media and Washington wanted us to believe. In this regard, in January 2012, the *Guardian* reported that a poll conducted by a Qatari foundation had found that, to its great surprise, some 55% of Syrians wanted al-Assad to stay in power, while most Arabs outside Syria were of the opinion that the President had to resign. NATO confirmed in June 2013 that this state of mind had hardly changed despite the escalation of the conflict. An internal study by the military alliance showed that 70% of the Syrian population supported the President while 20% adopted a neutral position.

The coalition's desire to topple al-Assad was as strong as the one it had felt in Libya against Gaddafi, with the difference that in Syria, the same coalition strengthened its alliance with Islamist governments to "clean up the mess", with this time Recep Tayyip Erdogan's Turkey on the front line. After all, when the first Syrian Army officers defected, they took refuge in Turkey, where they were welcomed with open arms by an Islamist country eager to do away with its secular neighbor. Backed by the Turkish intelligence service, the infamous MIT, the officers established the Free Syrian Army (FSA), to which Turkey offered hospitality and an operational base under the financial supervision of Saudi Arabia and Qatar. Military weapons and equipment were quickly supplied to the FSA after President Barack Obama had openly supported the new organization. It was at this time that the American services set up the famous "rat line", which consisted in getting hold of Gaddafi's arms stocks to transfer them to the Syrian rebels, who, for that matter, did not have to wait long: a former CIA counterterrorism specialist, Philip Giraldi, reported that "unmarked" NATO airplanes carrying weapons had been seen over Syria as early as December 2011. It was also known that volunteers from the Libyan National Transitional Council were dispatched to assist the rebels. Thus, NATO was already delivering weapons to the FSA at the end of 2011. Now, did the coalition intervene before that date? Yes, if we are to believe a former minister of Qatar, Hamad bin Jassim Jaber al-Thani. In an interview with Qatari TV, the man turned out to be quite talkative and revealed that his country, alongside Saudi Arabia, Turkey and the United States, had shipped weapons to jihadists as early as the beginning of the Arab

Spring in 2011. This brings us to ask a fundamental question: what was the extent of the arms transfers to the rebels?

The Memo That Could Have Turned Everything Around

Before we talk about arms trafficking, though, we need to open another parenthesis on Hillary Clinton. Because the former Secretary of State, as we already know, was perceived as a hawk within the White House. And as she had done in Libya, Clinton had been eager to promote a forceful intervention in Syria. This eagerness, it was learned later, drew its source in part from a message totally ignored by the mainstream media: a 1,200-word memo sent in April 2012 by James P. Rubin, a senior State Department diplomat under Bill Clinton, to then-Secretary of State Hillary Clinton. The memo's main topic was the balance of power in the Near East. Rubin, who was acting as a sort of advisor to Clinton, dismissed the idea that negotiating with Iran would stop the Islamist republic "from improving the crucial part of any nuclear weapons program—the capability to enrich uranium." The "advisor" was referring to the nuclear talks between Iran, the United States, the United Kingdom, France, China, Russia, and Germany, which would lead to the famous Vienna Agreement on the Iranian nuclear program signed in July 2015. Putting on the mask of Machiavelli, Rubin explained that if Iran succeeded in obtaining the nuclear bomb, Israel would suffer a strategic setback to the extent that it could no longer "respond to provocations with conventional military strikes on Syria and Lebanon, as it can today." If denied the ability to bomb as it pleases, Israel might then leave off secondary targets and strike at the main enemy instead, added Rubin. As a result, he continued—and this is where things get hairy—, the United States would have to topple Bashar al-Assad to weaken Iran and allay the fears of Israel. "Bringing down Assad would not only be a massive boon to Israel's security, it would also ease Israel's understandable fear of losing its nuclear monopoly", wrote Rubin. "Then, Israel and the United States might be able to develop a common view of when the Iranian program is so dangerous that military action could be warranted." Ironically, Rubin was, in fact, only following in the footsteps of the Bush administration by putting forward a project the latter did not have the time to initiate: destabilizing Iran by first attacking its great ally, Syria. The memo was quite clear: with the overthrow of al-Assad, "Iran would be strategically isolated, unable to exert its influence in the Middle East. The resulting regime in Syria will see the United States as a friend, not an enemy. Washington would gain substantial recognition as fighting for the people in the Arab world, not the corrupt regimes. For Israel, the rationale for a bolt from the blue attack on Iran's nuclear facilities would be eased. And a new Syrian regime might well be open to early action on the frozen peace talks with Israel. Hezbollah in Lebanon would be cut off from its Iranian sponsor since Syria would no longer be a transit point for Iranian training, assistance and missiles." So, these were "good reasons" to intervene in order to disrupt the Syrian regime. Rubin was convinced that this approach was inexpensive and profitable—as if war could prove to be inexpensive—, that it would eliminate one enemy, weaken two others and create such joy among ordinary Syrians that peace talks between Damascus and Tel Aviv would spring back to life. In short, the risks appeared to be nil. Hillary Clinton picked up the idea and began to lobby the White House for a ground intervention, but she was met with a flat refusal from President Obama. The relationship between these two central figures in the White House would never be the same afterwards; Clinton even resigned from her post as Secretary of State on February 1, 2013.

But we are not done yet with the former presidential candidate. In late 2009, she wrote a diplomatic memo, later released by Wikileaks, in which she argued that "donors in Saudi Arabia constitute the most significant source of funding to Sunni terrorist groups worldwide." This was a serious accusation, although well-founded. But she went further: "While the Kingdom of Saudi Arabia (KSA) takes seriously the threat of terrorism within [the country], it has been an ongoing challenge to persuade Saudi officials to treat terrorist financing emanating from Saudi Arabia as a strategic priority", she added in the secret memo. Moreover, "Saudi Arabia remains a critical financial support base for Al-Qaeda, the Taliban [...] and other terrorist groups, including Hamas, which probably raise millions of dollars annually from Saudi sources, often during Hajj and Ramadan." And about Qatar: "Qatar has adopted a largely passive approach to cooperating with the U.S. against terrorist financing. Qatar's overall level of [counterterrorism] cooperation with the U.S. is considered the worst in the region." Two years later during the Arab Spring, the former Secretary of State, despite her negative opinion about Saudi Arabia and Qatar, would rely upon those two countries to provide funds to rebels in Libya and Syria. Rebels who would also be able to count on the United States for the supply of weapons. End of the parenthesis.

The Pentagon Involved in Arms Trafficking

The Bush administration, as we have noted, used behind-the-scenes maneuvering to destabilize the Shiite community, in particular in Syria. But the destabilization effort did not stop in 2008 with George W. Bush's last mandate; the man who succeeded him in the Oval Office, in defiance of his ideological differences, felt it necessary to carry on the work of his predecessor. Days before violence erupted during the Arab Spring in Syria, *Reuters* reported that the Syrian security forces had seized a large shipment of weapons, explosives and night-vision goggles at the Al-Tanf border crossing in the Al-Anbar Governorate. A Saudi official, Anwar Eshki, later said to the *BBC* that his government had shipped arms to the al-Omari mosque in Daraa, long before all hell broke loose in the city. With that in mind, it is now possible to make the link between those arms transfers and the first demonstrations where armed civilians had fired on the Syrian forces. Let's recall the figures: during the first 10 to 12 months of the conflict, out of approximately 5,000 people who died during the protests, 478 were police officers and 2,091 were part of the military or the security forces.

Saudi Arabia, along with Qatar, provided the tokens needed to purchase and transport these weapons, but the CIA was the one to provide the logistics backstage. For the occasion, the agency, using shell companies, had hired retired U.S. soldiers to ship Gaddafi's weapons from Benghazi, Libya, to Syrian ports so that they could be redirected to the rebels. A declassified CIA document dated October 2012 disclosed the contents of a single shipment sent to the rebels at the end of August 2012: 500 assault rifles, 100 rocket-propelled grenades (RPG), 300 grenades and 400 howitzers. Each shipment could include up to ten containers, according to the document, each container being loaded with about 50,000 pounds of goods, which accounted for a total load of 250 tons of weapons per shipment. Even if the CIA had carried out only one operation per month, the deliveries would have totaled 2,750 tons of weapons from October 2011 to August 2012 alone. And as soon as Gaddafi's stocks ran out, the coalition turned to Eastern European countries for weapons procurement and shipping. Between 2012 and 2016, a dozen Eastern European states approved arms and ammunition exports worth €829 million, all intended for the Syrian rebels. Croatia was one of the first countries on this side of Europe to jump into the fray in the winter of 2012-2013. During a visit to Washington in the summer of 2012, a Croatian official offered the Americans to buy his country's stockpiles of old weapons dating back to the Soviet era. Then, as reported by *Balkan Insight*, "Zagreb was later put in touch with the Saudis, who bankrolled the purchases, while the CIA helped with logistics for an airlift that began late that year." According to the United Nations, in terms of ammunition alone, the Croatian state's export figures amounted to $36 million in the two years following the start of the Syrian conflict.

It was through *Operation Timber Sycamore*, launched in 2013, that the Balkan States supplied arms to Syrian rebels with the help of, among others, the CIA, always willing to act as the go-between. In 2015, *Timber Sycamore* took on its full meaning as the Islamic State swept Syria from north to south and from east to west. In December 2014, the Pentagon set up, this time, the *Train and Equip* program at a cost of $500 million to train a new force among the Syrian rebels, a force that would later get modern U.S.-made weapons. But nine months later, the program was halted, with only a handful of recruits having made it onto the battlefield. After facing a series of negative headlines, the Pentagon, in September 2015, shifted its focus from *Train and Equip* to *Timber Syca-*

more through the Eastern bloc, which was to become the new supplier of arms and ammunition to the Syrian opposition. The operation was in part run by the Special Operations Command (SOCOM), whose HQ was in Amman, Jordan. From the early days of *Timber Sycamore* until May 2017, the SOCOM purchased $240 million worth of arms and ammunition from Bulgaria, Bosnia and Herzegovina, the Czech Republic, Kazakhstan, Serbia, Poland, and Romania, according to the *Balkan Investigative Reporting Network* (*BIRN*) and the *Organized Crime and Corruption Reporting Project* (*OCCRP*), which looked through thousands of procurement records. Between December 2015 and September 2016, the same SOCOM chartered four cargo ships from Romanian and Bulgarian ports on the Black Sea; 6,300 tons of weapons and ammunition were thus delivered to military bases in Jordan but also in Turkey, the other logistics anchor point for supplying the Syrian rebels. The cargoes contained heavy machine guns, rocket launchers, anti-tank weapons, mortars, grenades, rockets, explosives, and ammunition. As in Iraq, the Americans were willing to make the most out of the war in Syria to "force-feed" their defense industry. But the SOCOM was not the only Pentagon department involved in arms transfer operations to this country. Picatinny Arsenal, a New Jersey military installation, was also part of the supply chain. At one point, Picatinny Arsenal acquired $480 million worth of Soviet-made weapons and ammunition from various countries. For a time, the American supplier could count on a colorful intermediary, the Swiss businessman Heinrich Thomet. With the help of Picatinny Arsenal, Thomet supplied both the Syrian rebels and the Afghan Army. This "middleman" was well known in the Pentagon as he had once found himself at the center of a scandal that had shaken the American defense headquarters and the Albanian government in 2008. In this military intrigue, the Swiss businessman was associated with Efraim Diveroli, an Israeli trafficker who won major contracts in 2006 to supply the U.S. Army with Chinese-made ammunition owned by the Albanian government. But because Chinese weapons and ammunition have been the subject of American sanctions since 1989 (when demonstrations in Tiananmen Square in Beijing were crushed by the Chinese government), Diveroli was sentenced to four years in prison in 2011 by the South District Court in Florida. Curiously, Thomet, who was at his side playing the intermediary role with Albanian officials, has never had to face justice. Yet, it was widely known that the Swiss businessman was on the CIA watch list for arms trafficking. Did he receive protection in high places that allowed him to evade justice? Just asking.

For the secret operations carried out under the umbrella of *Timber Sycamore*, the United States benefited from the services of an obscure company, Silk Way Airlines, from Azerbaijan. Silk Way was operating under the cover of diplomatic flights to transport arms from Eastern countries. This was a convenient process as diplomatic flights are exempt from taxes and control, which means that Silk Way's planes were able to freely transport hundreds of tons of weapons to different locations around the world without having to comply with regulations. Between 2014 and 2017, U.S. companies won billion-dollar contracts to resell "non-U.S. standard weapons" to whatever group or country that needed them. "Non-U.S. standard weapons" simply means that the hardware is considered unsafe and is prohibited in the United States; in other words, it poses a serious danger to anyone handling it. The private companies that provided those weapons all used Silk Way Airlines for their transportation. When the latter ran out of aircraft due to a busy schedule, the Azerbaijan Air Force took over. But whatever the carrier was, the cargoes never reached Azerbaijan. Everything was done on the sly in violation of the instructions provided in the end-user certificates. Here is an example: on May 12, 2015, an Azerbaijan Air Force plane carrying eighteen tons of grenade launchers departed from Burgas, Bulgaria, bound for the Nasosnaya Air Base, Azerbaijan. The American company behind the shipment was Purple Shovel, while the recipient was the Ministry of Defense of Azerbaijan. But the aircraft never made it to Nasosnaya. Instead, the cargo was unloaded at the U.S. military base in Incirlik, Turkey, then delivered to U.S.-supported rebel factions in Syria. There were many other examples of this type. In February and March 2017, Saudi Arabia received 350 tons of weapons through diplomatic flights from Silk Way Airlines. The cargoes included 37,350 pieces of 128 mm and 122 mm rockets. The provider was a front company called Tehnoremont Temerin, of

Serbia, and the recipient was Fameway Investment Ltd, of Cyprus, an island where meet all kinds of traffickers. It is obvious that the final destination of those weapons was Syria. To avoid the spotlights, the Pentagon needed to bring a variety of intermediaries together. We talked earlier about two of those middlemen, Heinrich Thomet and Efraim Diveroli. But another one is worth mentioning: Marc Morales, CEO of Global Ordnance. For a time, Morales and his company were among the major actors in the Pentagon's supply line. The head of Global Ordnance had been chosen despite being part of a group of 22 businessmen indicted by the U.S. Justice Department for trying to bribe the Minister of Defense of Gabon in the intention of obtaining a contract for 15 million dollars in an arms deal. The FBI had dismantled the network in 2010, but the charges were dropped in February 2012 as the juries were unable to reach a verdict on seven defendants—including Morales—during two separate trials, according to the *Balkan Investigative Reporting Network* (BIRN) and the *Organized Crime and Corruption Reporting Project* (OCCRP). The Justice Department, afterwards, took an unusual step: drop all charges against the 22 business managers due to criticism by the judge at the second trial, who pointed out "structural deficiencies" in the investigation. Now, as expected, the "non-U.S. standard weapons" that the American companies bought from Eastern countries ended up causing a tragedy. Three firms, Regulus Global, Purple Shovel and Skybridge Tactical, were sued over a fatal rocket explosion that occurred on June 6, 2015, at a shooting range in Anevo, Bulgaria. An instructor, Francis Norwillo, was killed during the incident, and others were injured. Norwillo was a U.S. Navy veteran who had just been hired by Skybridge Tactical for only a week and a half to train rebels in the handling of weapons. His widow claimed that Regulus Global, Purple Shovel and Skybridge Tactical provided old RPGs for testing even though they knew that these weapons had been rejected by the United States government that considered them "defective, unstable and dangerous", according to court documents. Regulus Global had entrusted a part of its work to Alguns Ltd, a company based in Sofia, Bulgaria. The owner of Alguns, Alexander Dimitrov, is a former business partner of a Bulgarian organized crime figure, Boyan Petrakiev, nicknamed "the Baron." Alguns was involved in six deliveries of Bulgarian-made unguided rocket-propelled grenade launchers using Ilyushin-76 aircraft, the flights of which took off from the U.S. base in Incirlik, Turkey, in May 2015.

As we have just shown, the Pentagon was not too fussy about the choice of the people and organizations it associated with, just as it did not care about the countries involved in its traffic. This was the case of Belarus, for instance, from which the U.S. Army bought 700 anti-tank missiles even though this country is on the list of the U.S. State Department that imposes restrictions on the arms trade. What happened next was highly predictable: the United States quickly lost control of the delivery of weapons in Syria, which was just a repetition of a scenario seen in Iraq and Libya years earlier. And as usual, the CIA was buried head first in the mud pool. Beginning in mid-June 2012, officers from the agency were secretly operating in southern Turkey to select rebel factions that would benefit from the American generosity. When asked about the matter, Washington officials were quick to point out that the CIA was very selective and that terrorist groups were excluded from any deal. These were, however, the same officials who later had to admit that most of the weapons that flowed into Syria ended up on the side of the rapidly growing branch of Al-Qaeda in the country, the Al-Nusra Front. In October 2012, a Syrian expert, Joshua Landis, brought up some figures: between 60% and 80% of the weapons the United States sent to Syria went to Al-Qaeda and its affiliated groups. Were these figures overvalued? Perhaps, but still, in the spring of 2014, some U.S.-made BGM-71 TOW anti-tank missiles, which came from the stock of 15,000 TOWs transferred to the Saudis a year earlier, began to appear in the hands of anti-Assad groups. The main problem was that several of these groups were highly likely to be taken over by the powerful Al-Nusra Front. No later than November 2014, two of them were precisely struck by the Syrian branch of Al-Qaeda; these two groups are Harakat Hazm and the Syrian Revolutionary Front, whose heavy weapons were all seized by the Al-Nusra Front that was quick to brag about its feat, showing pictures of its seizure on social networks. The situation was such that Robert Ford, former U.S. Ambassador to Syria, acknowledged that the United States had failed to fulfill its obligations in this regard. And as ridiculous as it may sound, at one point, troops supported by the CIA fought against other groups backed by the Pentagon. The CIA-supported Fursan al-Haq had been chased out of the town of Marea, some 25 miles north of the city of Aleppo, by the Pentagon-assisted Syrian Democratic Forces. Other skirmishes involving the two groups took place in Azaz.

Another important organization was on the Syrian front line at the time: the Islamic State of Iraq and the Levant, or ISIS, which had also obtained weapons from private dealers and the Free Syrian Army. Those weapons were mostly manufactured in the United States and had been brought into Iraq and Syria by private security firms. And just as some members of the Al-Nusra Front had done before, Islamic State fighters showed their "toys" on the Web, among others BGM-71 TOW missile systems, the same ones that had been sold to Saudi Arabia in 2013. It was also in 2013 that M79 anti-tank rockets, identical to those supplied by Saudi Arabia to the Free Syrian Army, had been transferred to the ISIS camp. It is through analysis of the rockets' serial numbers, discovered by Kurds in eastern Syria, that the UK-based Conflict Armament Research (CAR) was able to determine that they came from the CIA-Saudi weapons airlift program. One journalist, Jurgen Todenhofer, witnessed how the West had lost control of the flow of arms. Todenhofer spent ten days in the company of an ISIS unit and claimed to have seen Western-made weapons, originally supplied to the Free Syrian Army, in the hands of members of the terrorist group. Those arms transfers were facilitated by Turkey, Qatar, and Saudi Arabia, but also by another great ally of the United States: Jordan. A great ally and a great looter: several shipments of weapons were regularly stolen by Jordan's General Intelligence Directorate and sold back on the black market. The officers involved in the scam used the profits to buy luxury goods, including SUVs, media sources said. According to Jordanian officials, several intelligence officers were fired but their profits never confiscated. Rebels who bought these weapons sold them to local traffickers, who, in turn, sold them back to jihadist groups, including ISIS. One of those weapons, a Kalashnikov, wound up in the hands of Abu Anwar Zeid, the man who attacked, on November 9, 2015, the King

Abdullah II Operations Training Center (KASOTC), located in the outskirts of Amman. The attack left five people dead, including two American instructors. One of the Jordanian officers arrested during the investigation into the thefts of weapons, General Samih Battikhi, was once convicted of being part of a scheme to obtain bank loans of around $600 million for fake government contracts. Battikhi had made $25 million in that project, but luckily for him, he never had to answer for his actions: he was sentenced to eight years in prison, but the sentence was eventually reduced to four years, which had to be served in his villa in the seaside town of Aqaba.

Moderate Opposition? A Myth

In a classified document dated August 12, 2012, the Defense Intelligence Agency (DIA) revealed that the Pentagon foresaw the rise of an "Islamic State" in Syria, whose main consequence would be the [re]destabilization of neighboring Iraq. In that document, the DIA also mentioned that the insurgency in Syria had taken a "sectarian direction" by attracting "religious and tribal powers" of Sunni origin to its network. In a section titled "The Future Assumptions of the Crisis", the report predicted the survival of the al-Assad's regime, but anticipated a bleak future for Syria with a conflict that would inevitably escalate into a "proxy war." It is thus clear that the DIA knew as soon as the summer of 2012 what upcoming events in Syria would be like. It is true that the insurgency's increasing sectarianism in that country was easily predictable, firstly because the Iraqi and the Libyan experiences had set the table in this regard, secondly because the first insurgents were supported by Saudi Arabia and Qatar, two countries that, as we know, have greatly contributed to the emergence of Islamism and jihadism in the world. The director of the DIA at the time was Lieutenant General Michael Flynn, a center-right man whose political culture was closer to the Republicans than the Democrats. Flynn once told journalist Seymour Hersh: "If the American public saw the intelligence we were producing daily, at the most sensitive level, they would go ballistic." Flynn had also said that his agency had issued several warnings to the

Obama administration about the catastrophic consequences of the overthrow of al-Assad, but officials in Washington had totally ignored them. The Pentagon, which was firmly opposed to shipping weapons to the rebels, had then decided to play behind President Obama's back. Seymour Hersh reported that the generals had taken action against the extremists without going through political channels by providing military intelligence to the Russians, Israelis and Germans in the hope that it would be passed on to the Syrian Army and used against the common enemies, the Al-Nusra Front and the Islamic State. Why the Russians, the Israelis and the Germans? Because 1) Russia was a long-standing Syria ally and was worrying about the threat posed to its only base in the Mediterranean, in Tartus; 2) because Israel was concerned about the security of its borders; 3) because Germany feared what might happen among its population of six million Muslims if the Islamic State spread out.

To fight against al-Assad, Washington's politicos initially relied on the sole Free Syrian Army (FSA), which received their support from the very first gunshots of the insurgency. The FSA had been set up in July 2011 by Colonel Riad al-Asaad and a few other Syrian military defectors. At first, the movement was undoubtedly legitimate, but it grew too fast. As a result, it had to contend with the massive arrival of fighters close to Islamist factions. The first chief officers to be trained were confined to the Apaydin camp in Turkey, closely watched by the Turkish authorities and separated from the Syrian civilian refugees. Every move, act, or word was controlled, including interviews with journalists. In reality, what was emerging was a resistance lacking a true leader and made up of local fighters who shared only a few common goals. In other words, what was called the Free Syrian Army was anything but an army with a clear plan, loyal soldiers, and a well-organized command. Among U.S. politicians, some quickly understood that the FSA was a lame entity that brought together a collection of groups whose fighters did not hesitate to pledge their allegiance to the obscurantism prescribed by the apologists of a strict Islam. Jaysh al-Islam, for one, a group funded largely by Saudi Arabia, entered into a tactical alliance with the FSA in the Damascus region, but also occasionally fought alongside the Al-Nusra Front, directly linked, as we have seen, to Al-Qaeda. The former Jaysh al-Islam's leader, Zahran Alloush, was seen honoring the memory of Osama bin Laden in videos posted on the Web. Another leader associated with the FSA, Jamal Ma'arouf, from the Syrian Revolutionary Front, admitted to having fought in jihadist organizations, including the Al-Nusra Front. Viewed as a "moderate" by the U.S.-led coalition, Ma'arouf refused to let his men fight against Islamists. Another one, the head of Aleppo's military council for the FSA, Abdul Jabbar al-Oqaidi, was filmed in 2012 with Abu Jandal al-Masri, one of ISIS's leaders. Oqaidi, who had once met with Robert Ford, the former U.S. Ambassador to Syria, had requested help from ISIS in his battle against the regime. In September 2014, Bassel Idriss, one of the FSA's commanders, revealed that troops from his army had joined their forces with factions of the Islamic State and the Al-Nusra Front in the Qalamun mountains. An Islamic State commander, Abu al-Atheer, confirmed in an interview with the Al-Jazeera network that the FSA was supplying weapons to jihadist groups, including anti-air-craft missiles and Konkurs anti-tank weapons, and that his own group had obtained many of these weapons on the black market from the army of "moderates."

Journalist Theo Padnos, who was held hostage by the Al-Nusra Front, added a layer of transparency to the matter when he said that each time he managed to escape, men from the FSA turned him over to his torturers. Even the very liberal *Washington Post* gave a surprising demonstration of honesty on August 18, 2014, when it compared the FSA to the army of Afghan mujahideen that had turned against its American sponsors after the armed conflict with the Soviet Union in the 1980s. The newspaper quoted Abu Yusaf, an ISIS commander: "In the East of Syria, there is no Free Syrian Army any longer" because "all Free Syrian Army people [there] have joined the Islamic State." Yusaf went on to say that among those who abandoned the FSA ship, many had been trained by the Americans, the British, the Turks, and the French. The U.S. intelligence was well aware of that problem, as pointed out by another source from the *Post*: "We had, in the early stages, information that radical groups had used the vacuum of the Arab Spring, and that some of the people the U.S. and their allies had trained to fight for 'democracy' in Libya and Syria had a jihadist agenda—already or later, [when they] joined Al-Nusra or the Islamic State." Other groups supported by the West have raised controversy, among others Ahrar al-Sham and the Army of Conquest. Before the rise of ISIS, Ahrar al-Sham was the largest military force in opposition to the al-Assad regime, with around 15,000 soldiers. Experts who followed its expansion never dared to call it a jihadist organization because, they said, it showed no interest in terrorist actions against Western countries. Perhaps not, but one thing is sure: some of its senior leaders had ties to jihadists and worked closely with the Al-Nusra Front. Ahrar al-Sham not only helped the Front take control of the Idlib governorate in 2015 but also joined this organization in an offensive south of the city of Aleppo in early April 2016, in violation of the ceasefire. But here's the thing: in Washington, the mood was predominantly indulgent toward Ahrar al-Sham, so much so that President Obama received with great pomp the organization's director of "foreign affairs", Labib al-Nahhas. A visit totally ignored by the mainstream media; only *McClatchy News Service* had reported it. Given the highly restrictive travel policy of the United States, granting a visa to a senior Ahrar al-Sham official for a visit to Washington takes on an obvious political significance. In fact, Labib al-Nahhas had previously met in Istanbul with the U.S. special envoy for Syria, Michael Ratney, and the State Department had decided to include his organization among the opposition groups invited to participate in a conference in Riyadh. That conference, organized by the United States with its regional allies, "was aimed at reaching agreement on the representation of opposition groups at political talks to be held with the [al-]Assad regime", according to the independent investigative journalist Gareth Porter. The Ahrar al-Sham representative showed up at the event as planned but left "after complaining that the results did not sufficiently reflect Ahrar's insistence that the opposition should have a Muslim identity." Ironically, it was the Russians, not the Americans, who responded to Ahrar al-Sham's arrogance by proposing that it be blacklisted and kept out of all ceasefire agreement. This would have had serious consequences for the organization since it would have been vulnerable to targeted attacks. Unsurprisingly, the Obama administration rejected the Russian proposal.

As for the Army of Conquest, or Jaish al-Fatah, it did not have better press. A source within the Saudi royal family involved in defense and security matters and quoted by *Middle East Eye* revealed that 90% of Army of Conquest's combatants were former Al-Nusra Front and Ahrar al-Sham members. No wonder, therefore, that in early 2015, Turkey, along with Saudi Arabia and Qatar, helped plan an Army of Conquest offensive in the Idlib Governorate. The Saudis, disappointed by the Free Syrian Army, had thrown themselves in the arms of the Army of Conquest as they had no other option, they said at the time. On his side, the Turkish President, Recep Tayyip Erdogan, had a very clear position in this regard: since the West had refused to intervene directly in Syria and impose a no-fly zone over the country, it was then up to the States in the region to conduct the operations, no matter who the "subcontractors" were. Plagued by internal conflicts, the Army of Conquest practically dissolved in the fall of 2015. Another group, the CIA-backed Southern Front, fought alongside Al-Nusra during the campaign to take the city of Daraa in June 2015. Yet, the Southern Front was described as a non-hardline Islamist rebel organization that rejected extremism. Talking about the CIA, a commander of the Fursan ul-Haq, a rebel group that had received TOW missiles through the agency's channels, had explained that world powers misunderstood an important fact, that is, they needed to "work" with the Al-Nusra Front and other Islamist groups to fight both the al-Assad regime and the Islamic State. This man had the merit of being honest.

Saudi Arabia's Double Game

"Our biggest problem was our allies. The Turks [...], the Saudis, the Emirates [...] what were they doing? They were so determined to take down [the Syrian President Bashar al-]Assad and essentially have a proxy Sunni-Shia war, what did they do? They poured hundreds of millions of dollars and tens, thousands of tons of weapons into anyone who would fight against Assad." Those wise words had been spoken in

October 2014 by then-U.S. Vice President Joe Biden as he answered a question from a student at the Harvard Kennedy School. The allies that Biden had referred to were not only Turkey, Saudi Arabia and the United Arab Emirates, but also Qatar; all these countries have never been shy to partner with obscure organizations whose sole purpose was to defeat the secular government of Bashar al-Assad to subsequently impose a shariah-based society in Syria. And one of these countries, Saudi Arabia, has always made it a point of encouraging the spread of Islam around the world.

In Washington, the attacks of September 11, 2001, bring back painful memories; above all, they remind U.S. officials that their Wahhabi ally has appeared too often in investigation documents. The current king himself, Salman bin Abdulaziz Al Saud, has a roadmap that raises many questions. Intelligence services have accumulated a wealth of information about the man, which information needs to be put into perspective to better understand what is at stake. The king's escapades date back long before he acceded to the throne. We owe the Russians a report that revealed that on June 22, 1998, a hundred Chechen fighters close to Al-Qaeda had been transported to a secret military camp located not too far from Riyadh, the Saudi capital, where they had obtained a four-month training in explosives, unarmed combat and the handling of small arms. When not in training, the Chechens learned Wahhabism, the master doctrine of Saudi Islam. More intriguing, the Russian report did not fail to mention the name of the camp's sponsor: Salman bin Abdulaziz Al Saud. In 1992, Salman, then-governor of the province of Riyadh, was appointed by King Fahd to found and run the Saudi High Commission for Aid to Bosnia (SHC), an organization that had successfully amassed over $600 million a decade later. This was before NATO forces raided its Sarajevo offices, which enabled them to discover various photographs of government buildings in Washington, the World Trade Center before and after the 2001 attacks, the American embassies in Nairobi and Dar es Salaam (attacked in 1998), and the USS Cole, an American destroyer that was also the target of an attack in October 2000. Detailed reports of meetings attended by Osama bin Laden were also found within the SHC's Bosnia offices. It was estimated at the time that approximately $41 million had gone missing from the organization's coffers. In 2008, in an aborted lawsuit against the Saudi government, the families of the victims of 9/11, through their lawyers, questioned an Al-Qaeda agent who had confirmed that the Saudi High Commission had provided cash, weapons and vehicles to members of the bin Laden clan. According to court documents filed by the same lawyers, the SHC had also contributed to the financing of Al-Qaeda camps in Afghanistan, where the hijackers had received their training for the 2001 attacks. The Defense Intelligence Agency (DIA), for its part, accused the Saudi organization of supporting Mohamed Farrah Aidid, a Somali warlord whose followers were responsible for the deaths of eighteen American soldiers in 1993. The SHC was finally closed down in 2011. European documents also showed that Salman shelled out $120 million directly from his bank accounts to finance another organization, the Third World Relief Agency, which we know was used, among other things, to fill the coffers of Islamist fighters in Bosnia. And in November 2002, the current king sponsored a fund-raiser organized in honor of three other charities suspected of having had ties with terrorism: the International Islamic Relief Organization, the Al-Haramain Foundation, and the World Assembly of Muslim Youth. Criticized in the West for his doubtful relationships, Salman replied that it was not the kingdom's fault if criminals diverted charitable funds toward terrorist objectives. A sure way of clearing his conscience. The king also played an important role in the Abd al-Aziz bin Baz Foundation, named after an important Saudi mufti who died in 1999. The foundation's website is specific: it benefited from the direct and uninterrupted support of Salman since its creation in 2001. During his lifetime, Abd al-Aziz bin Baz had wanted to turn Saudi Arabia into a fundamentalist stronghold close to the Islamist aims of Osama bin Laden. With regard to women, the late mufti had declared that those who expressed a desire to study alongside men in schools and universities across the country were nothing else than "prostitutes." One of the foundation's board members, Aidh bin Abdullah al-Qarni, is a notorious anti-Semite. He once said to the Palestinians, "[t]hroats must be slit and skulls must be shattered", in reference to their battle against Israelis. Another religious leader close to Salman, Saleh al-Maghamsi, once stated that since Osama bin Laden was a Muslim, he had more "holiness and honor" in the eyes of Allah than Jews and Christians. Even after making those comments, al-Maghamsi continued to receive the support of Salman, who was appointed chairman of the board of directors of a research center in Medina run by none other than al-Maghamsi himself. Salman also sponsored and attended a cultural festival organized by the religious leader.

Many cases related to Saudi Arabia remain unclear to this day. Still, no wealthy Saudi businessman or member of the royal caste has so far had to face justice since 9/11. We could mention, for instance, the case of two Saudis who, according to an American intelligence report, made about twenty payments between November 2001 and January 2002, totaling one million dollars, to an Al-Qaeda official responsible for facilitating the escape of some of Osama bin Laden's accomplices. There is also this former head of Islamic Affairs at the Saudi Embassy in Berlin, Mohamed Fakihi, whose business card had been discovered during a search in the apartment of Mounir el-Motassadeq, an Al-Qaeda asset who was released in October 2018 after spending 15 years in prison for assisting the hijackers of the Hamburg cell. Fakihi admitted to being sympathetic to Osama bin Laden and to pulling money out of the embassy to finance Al-Qaeda-linked mosques and charities. A source connected to the German investigation said that more than $800,000 had vanished from the coffers of the Islamic Affairs Department of the Saudi Embassy in Berlin. Fakihi has never been tried and had no problem returning to Saudi Arabia. Another case is that of a former Saudi Ambassador to Pakistan who allegedly met with Nasiruddin Haqqani, a former high-ranking member of the Al-Qaeda-affiliated Haqqani network. Everyone in the U.S. intelligence community knew that Taliban and Haqqani emissaries were regularly traveling to Saudi Arabia to raise funds. In this respect, Agha Jan Motasim, a former member of the Taliban government in Afghanistan, asserted that between 2002 and 2007, so after the 2001 attacks that had placed his organization on the second podium of terrorism behind Al-Qaeda, he was one of those emissaries who would go to Saudi Arabia two or three times a year for financial reasons. Another case involves an individual by the name of Fahad Abdullah Saleh Bakala, who used to be the Saudi royal family's official pilot at the same time that he was, according to the FBI, in close contact with two hijackers, Ahmed and Hamza al-Ghamdi. It is rumored that he flew Osama bin Laden from Saudi Arabia to Afghanistan. The Saudis have never given any explanations about those events nor about this Riyadh-based company named Twaik Group, which had deposited more than $250,000 in bank accounts under the management of Mamoun Darkazanli, a Syrian businessman who used to belong to the Al-Qaeda cell in Hamburg. According to the *Chicago Tribune*, the German authorities had discovered in 2004 that Twaik Group was serving as a cover for the Saudi intelligence agency. Before the September 11 attacks, two of the company's executives had been suspected of doing some work for Al-Qaeda. In addition, one of Twaik Group's employees, Reda Seyam, was accused of playing a role in financing the 2002 Bali bombings.

It was predictable that in Syria, Saudi Arabia would not remain neutral in a conflict that was taking place a few stadiums away from its backyard. Especially since it has never intended to give up on its project of religious and political hegemony in the Middle East. It is no secret that the Al-Nusra Front's and the Islamic State's ideological foundations were drawn from the frameworks of Wahhabism. Books of Wahhabi scholars have circulated and are still circulating among jihadist groups mobilized in conflict zones. According to *The Economist*, twelve Saudi judges administered the Islamic courts in Raqqa when the city was under ISIS control. Of greater concern is that the Saud's religious domination is not felt only in the Middle East. In 2007, Saudi Arabia was spending $2 billion promoting its extremist movement, a figure that had increased twofold in 2015. Indian intelligence agencies reported that between 2011 and 2013, the Saudis sent $250 million and dispatched thousands of preachers to India to establish mosques and set up Wahhabi seminars. In the United Kingdom, the number of mosques adhering to Salafism and Wahhabism was 68 in 2007, but 110 in 2015. Some of those mosques are directly managed from Saudi Arabia, including the King Fahd mosque in Edinburgh. Other revealing figures: a 2010 *BBC* survey showed that around 5,000

British children in some 40 clubs and schools were trained as part of Saudi Arabia's official curriculum. In the United States, 80% of the 1,200 mosques were built after 2001, most often with Saudi funding. In 2013, 75% of Islamic centers in North America relied on Wahhabi preachers. Many of them promote anti-Western ideas through their sermons and materials provided by the Saudi government. An example: a text written by Saudi technocrats for grade 10 students called *Science of Tawheed*, copies of which were discovered at the Masjid el-Farouq mosque in Houston, teaches that if a Muslim "thinks it is permissible to be under [the] control [of the Westerners] and [that] he is pleased with the way they are, then there is no doubt that he is no longer a Muslim." In Canada, Saudis have made donations to Islamic schools and mosques in Ottawa, Mississauga, Scarborough and Quebec City, among other places. At the Salaheddin Islamic Center, in Scarborough (province of Ontario), a preacher by the name of Aly Hindy, whose salary is said to be partly paid by the Saudi government, had declared in a speech that homosexuality was a pure invention and that the 9/11 attacks had been a CIA operation. Hindy had refused to join other imams to sign a declaration condemning the 2005 London bombings. He also praised the "Toronto 18", the 18 terrorists who had planned to carry out attacks against the Canadian Parliament and the Canadian Security Intelligence Service (CSIS) headquarters. When Mohamed Mahjoub, a former member of the Egyptian terrorist group Vanguards of Conquest, sought to be released from prison, Hindy had volunteered as his guarantor, a proposal that had been rejected by a judge. One of the founders of the Salaheddin Islamic Center where Hindy preaches, Hassan Farhat, left Canada to join an Al-Qaeda-linked group in Iraq, where he commanded a suicide bomber squad. Ahmed Khadr, formerly from Al-Qaeda and the father of Omar Khadr who received $10.5 million from the Canadian government as compensation after being detained in Guantanamo, attended the Salaheddin Islamic Center when he lived in Toronto. In Kosovo, after the war that ravaged the ex-Yugoslavia in the 1990s, Saudi Arabia undertook a spiritual conquest, where Islam was once considered very moderate. But in recent years, the Kosovar police have identified 314 residents—including two suicide bombers—who left the country to join ISIS, the highest number *per capita* in Europe. More and more Kosovars are radicalized and recruited by clandestine associations and extremist preachers funded mainly by Saudi Arabia. At the time of this writing, the Kosovan authorities had laid charges against 67 people, arrested 14 imams and closed down 19 Muslim organizations for hate speech and recruitment for terrorist operations. Almost all of them were in contact with Saudis.

Saudi Arabia, along with Turkey and Qatar, got involved from the start in the Syrian conflict by providing funds and weapons to the rebels, but that support did not dry up in the years that followed. The goal, it must be recalled, had been set from the first days of the protests: the al-Assad regime had to fall, and all means were good to carry through this project. According to *The Intercept*, on March 18, 2013, fighters from the Free Syrian Army launched multiple rocket attacks on different targets in the heart of Damascus, namely the Presidential Palace, the Damascus International Airport and a government security complex. We later learned that the FSA had received orders from Prince Salman bin Sultan of Saudi Arabia to "light up Damascus" and to "flatten" the Syrian capital's international airport, as reported in a document from the National Security Agency (NSA) released by the whistleblower Edward Snowden. By this act, the kingdom had found a way of celebrating the second anniversary of the Syrian "revolution." Salman bin Sultan had supplied 120 tons of explosives and other types of weapons to the opposition forces. The NSA document not only confirmed that the assault occurred but also specified that the Saudi government was "very pleased" with the outcome. A disturbing fact: it also revealed a prior knowledge of the attack among American intelligence, which had been warned by the Saudis. And it is very likely that Washington was tipped off about the Saudi government's plans, which implies that the Obama administration gave its tacit approval for the attack. Two thousand thirteen was also the year when divisions between Saudi Arabia and Qatar deepened over the conflict in Syria. The Saudis and Qataris, each on their side, increased significantly the number of flights of military cargo planes going to Turkey in December 2012 and kept up that pace during the following months. *The New York Times* reported a total of 160 such flights until mid-March 2013.

In January 2014, brought to despair over the lack of progress in the Syrian conflict, the director of the CIA, John Brennan, had summoned the heads of the intelligence services of Qatar and Saudi Arabia to a secret meeting in Washington in an attempt to persuade them to stop supporting extremist fighters in Syria. "The Saudis told us they were happy to listen, so everyone sat around in Washington to hear Brennan tell them that they had to get on board with the so-called moderates", a source told American journalist Seymour Hersh. "His message was that if everyone in the region stopped supporting Al-Nusra and ISIS, their ammunition and weapons would dry up, and the moderates would win out." Not surprisingly, Brennan's message was ignored by Riyadh and Doha.

If the Saudis had limited themselves to playing war games, we would have understood that their involvement in the Syrian conflict was part of the logic of defending geopolitical interests. But the princes did not just provide arms and funds to the rebels, they also took advantage of female slaves. At least that's what the *Sun Online* newspaper reported. A member of the Iraqi group Al-Hashd al-Shaabi is said to have acquired photographs taken from a Yazidi slave market in Saudi Arabia, which had first appeared on a mobile phone belonging to an ISIS fighter. Thousands of Yazidis were kidnapped by ISIS troops and sold on the slave market. According to a UN report, the price of these Yazidi slaves ranged from $40 to $160.

Qatar's Double Game

Early in the Syrian conflict until 2013, Qatar was the rebels' leading financial backer, contributing $3 billion, according to the *Financial Times*. It is also the country that made the largest arms transfers: 70 cargo aircraft flights between April 2012 and March 2013, revealed the Stockholm International Peace Research Institute. As it happens, the majority of those arms ended up in the jihadist camp. It is no coincidence that men from the Al-Nusra Front set out for Doha in 2012 to attend meetings with senior military and financial officials in Qatar, if we rely on the *Wall Street Journal*. All these facts did not escape a Western diplomat—whose name was not disclosed—stationed in the Qatari capital who said that "eight to twelve personalities in Qatar" were collecting funds for the jihadists, among others the Al-Nusra Front and the Islamic State. Qatar, more than any other country in the Middle East, wanted the downfall of the Bashar al-Assad's regime. It is the main reason why the dictator's hold on power has been met with anger in Doha. And what further angered the Qataris is that they were publicly blamed for funding terrorist groups. At the forefront of the accusers: Qatar's neighbor, Saudi Arabia. One can easily imagine the long, tense faces in the back rooms of the imperial palace in Doha when one of the main backers of Islamic fundamentalism accuses your government of being a funds provider for terrorist groups. The irony is that this competitor, despite its flaws, was right. In all likelihood, Qatar has become the number one sponsor of international terrorism. Journalist and political writer Kenneth Timmerman knows a great deal about it. In 1998, Timmerman spent some time in London as a contributor to *Reader's Digest* to work on an article on Osama bin Laden. During his stay in the British capital, he had learned that Al-Qaeda was receiving payments directly from the Qatar Embassy. The Qatari government had reportedly instructed the Embassy staff to hand over suitcases of cash to bin Laden's agents every week. Faced with the rise of Al-Qaeda, the emirate was visibly seeking to protect itself from terrorist attacks. That would explain why Doha concluded an agreement with the Islamist organization, which agreement was renewed in 2003, according to the *Sunday Times*. The money the royal family poured into the coffers of Al-Qaeda was allegedly used, among other things, to finance the group's activities in Iraq. An Iraqi government source, quoted by the *Sunday Times*, not only confirmed this information but also said that the agreement was renewed once again in March 2005 after a suicide bombing hit a theater in Doha, killing a British professor. Some might be inclined to give Qatar the benefit of the doubt: wouldn't the Qatari sheikhs simply want to live in peace? By accepting this assertion, one would show too much leniency toward the world's largest exporter of natural gas, as its road is too winding for anyone to ascribe good intentions to its leaders. A road whose construction did not begin in

1998 with the funds secretly paid to Al-Qaeda, but in 1995 when the United States had just found a man they considered potentially danger-ous. His name: Khalid Sheikh Mohammed.

At the time, American intelligence already knew that Sheikh Moham-med was the uncle of Ramzi Yousef, the instigator of the first attack on the World Trade Center in 1993, and that he had participated in the planning of the Bojinka plot that involved the hijacking of eleven American airplanes to blow them up in midair. Bojinka was, so to speak, the forerunner of 9/11. It had been foiled thanks to the vigilance of the Philippine authorities, but it was only a temporary setback for Khalid Sheikh Mohammed and his entourage. Melissa Boyle Mahle, a former CIA case officer within the Middle East division, was the one who had been tasked with tracking down Sheikh Mohammed, which she did in 1995 in a country, Qatar, curiously seen as an ally of the United States in the war on terror. Mahle had then suggested to her superiors that they transfer the terrorist through the process of extraordinary rendi-tion, that is, "outside the scope of the normal judicial structures." But Washington preferred to file a request with the Qatari authorities to start the extradition procedures. Louis Freeh, then-director of the FBI, had sent a message to Doha asking for permission to transfer their man to the United States. A move the director probably regretted because Qatar, without openly admitting it, never considered turning Sheikh Mohammed over to the American authorities, even after receiving a formal request from them for extradition. Warned by high-ranking figures of the Qatari royal family, Sheikh Mohammed went off the radar. These high-ranking figures were Hamad bin Jassim bin Jaber al-Thani, former Minister of Foreign Affairs of Qatar, Abdullah bin Khalid bin Hamad al-Thani, Minister of the Interior, as well as Abdul Karim al-Thani, another member of the ruling family. All three were close to the mastermind of the 9/11 attacks. Abdul Karim al-Thani would later protect another important figure in the jihadist move-ment: Abu Musab al-Zarqawi, the man who was to become the leader of Al-Qaeda's Iraqi branch. Al-Zarqawi had left Qatar with a Qatari passport and a million dollars in cash. Another former CIA case officer, Robert Baer, corroborated the allegations about the ties that bound the Qatari family to Khalid Sheikh Mohammed. In December 1997, Baer had met with Hamad bin Jassim bin Hamad al-Thani, a former minister of Economy and Trade in the Qatari government who, back then, was in exile following an abortive coup in 1996. Al-Thani had told Baer that Sheikh Mohammed had maintained good relations with several members of the royal family, including Abdullah bin Khalid bin Hamad al-Thani. According to the former minister of Economy and Trade, when agents of the Qatar Ministry of Interior had learned that the FBI had succeeded in finding Sheikh Mohammed, they had made sure to suppress all evidence of his presence in the offices of the police academy, in Doha, as well as in the Ministry of Water and Electricity and in a farm where he had spent some time. Worse still, while on the run after 9/11, Sheikh Mohammed returned to Qatar, where he stayed for two weeks, according to a Saudi intelligence source quoted by *The New York Times* in a 2003 article. Another article in the same newspaper reported that Abdullah bin Khalid bin Hamad al-Thani had sheltered, in all, a good hundred extremists on his lands, including ten members of Al-Qaeda who were on the FBI's most-wanted list. Less fortunate than Khalid Sheikh Mohammed, Ahmed Hikmat Shakir, a former employee of the Ministry of Endowments and Islamic Affairs, was arrested by the Qatari authorities six days after 9/11 because he was said to be close to two of the hijackers. When the police searched Shakir's apartment, they discovered documents relating to the 1993 World Trade Center bombings, the Bojinka plot, the bombings of two American embassies in Africa, and the attack on the USS Cole in the port of Aden, Yemen. But while the FBI announced its intention to interrogate Shakir, Doha quickly released him without any explanation.

So, as early as the mid 1990s, Qatar was protecting terrorists in full view of the American government. But it did more than protecting them. Jamal al-Fadl, an Al-Qaeda defector who went into exile in the United States in 1996, told the American authorities that Osama bin Laden had confessed to him that the royal family-linked Qatar Charitable Society (now Qatar Charity) was one of the main sources of funding for Al-Qaeda. According to al-Fadl, one of the former directors of the Qatar Charity was also a member of the terrorist organization. That former director had provided, among other things, funds and travel documents to fighters in Eritrea, as well as $20,000 to another organization that was planning an attack in Sudan. Osama bin Laden himself is alleged to have visited Qatar at least twice between 1996 and 2000, at a time when he was already appearing in U.S. intelligence services records. A Defense Department letter submitted to the Congress in 2003 pointed out that the ex-leader of Al-Qaeda visited Doha from January 17 to 19, 1996, where there was talk on operations targeting American and British interests in Dammam, Dhahran and Khobar, Saudi Arabia. Were members of the royal family part of the discussions? Knowing that Al-Qaeda's coffers were empty after bin Laden left Sudan, can we suggest that the Qataris had given him some cash? The question is worth asking since U.S. intelligence knew very well that before and after 9/11, Al-Qaeda was receiving money on a regular basis from rich donors from the Gulf, above all Qatar, as we have previously seen. Ayman al-Zawahiri, who succeeded bin Laden as the head of Al-Qaeda, also spent some time in Qatar, as did Mohammed Atef, the organization's former military chief who died in November 2001 in a U.S. airstrike in Afghanistan. It seems that the tiny emirate takes pleasure in offering hospitality to fugitives if only to thumb its nose at the Americans. In the moments following the Saddam Hussein's fall in March 2003, Sajida Khairallah Talfah, the widow of the former Iraqi strongman, fled to Qatar. Fled is not quite the right word we should use, though, because Talfah had been invited, along with her daughter, by the country's Deputy Prime Minister. She still lives there, in defiance of an Interpol arrest warrant and despite the fact that her name appears on Baghdad's most wanted list. Sajida Khairallah Talfah has been accused of providing money to Iraqi insurgents, including members of Al-Qaeda's branch in Iraq, according to a report released in October 2007 by the United States Congressional Research Service. The Iraqi government made an extradition request to Qatar, to no avail.

Let's recall what a Western diplomat based in Doha said: at one point, "eight to twelve personalities in Qatar" collected funds for the jihadists, among others for the Al-Nusra Front and the Islamic State. That diplomat was partly right, only he had underestimated the number of Qatari personalities who do not bother concealing their liking for Islamists. Among them: the al-Marri brothers, who had been detained separately shortly after 9/11 for their involvement in Al-Qaeda. One of them, Ali Saleh Kahlah al-Marri, had been chosen by Khalid Sheikh Mohammed to become an Al-Qaeda sleeping agent on American soil. His task was to plan attacks on water tanks and the New York Stock Exchange building, among other targets. He was taken into detention in Guantanamo in connection with these events, but was repatriated to Qatar on January 18, 2015, as part of a prisoner swap between the United States and the Qatari government. Upon his return to Qatar, he was considered a true hero and even received calls from government officials. The fact that the Americans agreed to deliver Ali Saleh Kahlah al-Marri to the Qatari authorities is rather appalling. Perhaps the emirate's flat refusal to hand over his bank records to the U.S. authorities in 2008 was already forgotten in Washington. As for Al-Marri's younger brother, Jaralla Saleh Mohammed Kahla al-Marri, he had trained in an Al-Qaeda camp in Afghanistan before 9/11 and was suspected of sending 10,000 dollars as "operational funds" to his brother. He was nonetheless repatriated to Qatar much earlier than Ali, in July 2008 to be exact, after the Qatari government promised the Americans that it would not allow him to travel abroad. It was a false promise: in early 2009, al-Marri turned up in the United Kingdom, where he was seen in a conference tour with another ex-Guantanamo prisoner, Moazzam Begg. The U.S. Ambassador to Qatar had concluded that Jaralla al-Marri's trip to the UK was "almost certainly" the result of a deliberate decision involving the government of the tiny Gulf state. The brother was finally arrested by the British authorities during his second visit to the United Kingdom.

This brings us to talk about Qatar's activities during the Syrian conflict. As we have seen, a large part of the sums paid to armed groups came from Qatar. And at the center of this funds transfer was a close friend of the royal family: Abd Al-Rahman Omeir al-Nuaimi, whom the United States placed on its list of sponsors of terrorism. Al-Nuaimi, who used to be president of the Qatar Football Association and an employee of the Ministry of Education, was charged by the United

States with transferring two million dollars a month to Al-Qaeda allies in Iraq, Syria, and Yemen. He also reportedly sent $576,000 to Abu Khalid al-Suri, one of the founders of Ahrar al-Sham, an Islamist group, and funded at least two other organizations associated with Al-Qaeda: Al-Shabaab, from Somalia, to which he provided $250,000, and Asbat al-Ansar, from Lebanon. Al-Nuaimi was also a founding member of the Association Eid bin Mohammed Al Thani, which appeared several times in the investigations of the American authorities. In 2010, the association had staged an event in Yemen along with Abdul Majeed al-Zindani, labeled a "Specially Designated Global Terrorist" by the United States. Representatives of the Qatar Embassy in Sanaa and the Qatari Ministry of Endowments and Islamic Affairs were among the attendees. Abd al-Wahhab Muhammad Abd al-Rahman al-Humayqani, who was accused of providing financial support to Al-Qaeda in the Arabian Peninsula (AQAP), received funds from the Association Eid bin Mohammed Al Thani, at a time when he was, in parallel, working for the Ministry of Endowments and Islamic Affairs.

To get back to Abd Al-Rahman Omeir al-Nuaimi, the man was arrested in June 1998 and detained without trial for almost three years for defying the Qatari authorities. Paradoxically, at the time of his release, he was received by the Emir himself, who had referred to him as an old friend. Al-Nuaimi was later appointed president of the Arab Center for Research and Policy Studies, an organization believed to be state-funded. The center's current director-general, Azmi Bishara, was able to obtain the Qatari citizenship after fleeing his homeland, Israel, just when he was suspected of selling state secrets to Hezbollah. Bishara was portrayed as a "court intellectual in Doha", where he advises the government on Syrian, Libyan, and Palestinian politics. Abdul Rahman Omeir al-Nuaimi also worked for the Global Anti-Aggression Coalition (GAAC), an NGO that, based on its name, advocates non-violence. Yet, it held at least one conference to support the "resistance" in Iraq, Somalia, and Gaza, resistance that al-Nuaimi proved himself to be the standard-bearer in 2008 when he published, from Doha, a statement on behalf of the GAAC that argued in favor of an insurrection against Israel. In 2009, al-Nuaimi championed an even more radical position by submitting, alongside radical clerics from the the Gulf, a petition that called for Muslims to kill Jews and seize their property. At a GAAC summit in 2010, our man was accompanied by Harith al-Dhari, accused by the United States of being an Al-Qaeda financier in Iraq. Another organization co-founded by al-Nuaimi called Al-Karama had forced the United Nations Working Group on Arbitrary Detention to put pressure on the United Arab Emirates to release Hassan al-Diqqi, the head of the Al-Ummah Party, banned in that country. Al-Diqqi had taken over Al-Ummah's leadership after the death of Mohammed al-Abduli, killed in 2013 while fighting in Syria with the troops of the Al-Nusra Front. The new leader himself had appeared in a video shot in a training camp for jihadists in Syria. On his Twitter account, he had urged the Muslim Brotherhood, Al-Qaeda and Salafists in general to jointly establish an Islamic nation whose objective would be to destroy Christians, Jews, and Persians. One of Al-Karama's founders, Hakem Obaysan al-Hamid al-Mutairi, provided funds to jihadist militias in Syria, including the Al-Nusra Front, Jund al-Aqsa, and Liwa al-Ummah (not to be confused with the Al-Ummah Party). After the death of Osama bin Laden in May 2011, al-Mutairi issued a message celebrating the former Al-Qaeda leader for his jihad against the West. In July 2008, Washington imposed sanctions on another Qatari, Khalifa Muhammad Turki al-Subaiy, a former senior official at the Central Bank of Qatar. According to the U.S. Treasury Department, al-Subaiy provided financial support to Khalid Sheikh Mohammed and other Al-Qaeda leaders in Pakistan, which was why he had been imprisoned for six months in Qatar. On October 10, 2008, the UN Security Council added al-Subaiy to its Al-Qaeda blacklist, which requires member states to freeze the assets of the individuals who appear on it. No surprise, Qatar has yet to make a move in that direction. In mid-2012, al-Subaiy sent hundreds of thousands of dollars and euros to Al-Qaeda in Pakistan, again according to the U.S. Treasury Department, and later solicited donations to help the same organization in Syria. Al-Subaiy also worked with Abd al-Malik Muhammad Yusuf Uthman Abd al-Salam, also known as Omar al-Qatari, another activist under sanctions by both the United States and the UN for providing financial and material support to Al-Qaeda in Pakistan and Syria. In May 2012, Al-Qatari, who was on his way to Qatar, was arrested by Lebanese authorities while carrying funds for the Al-Nusra Front. He was working at the time with Abdulaziz bin Khalifa al-Attiyah, cousin of the current Minister of Defense of Qatar. Al-Attiyah has made no effort to conceal his sympathies for Osama bin Laden, posting pictures of the former Al-Qaeda leader on his Twitter account, calling on God to "have mercy on our sheikh, Abu Abdallah", one of the nicknames given to bin Laden by his admirers. He also released a video promoting a fundraising campaign called Madid Ahl al-Sham, which used to serve as a conduit for financial assistance to the Al-Nusra Front and Hamas. Like al-Qatari, Al-Attiyah was also arrested in Lebanon for providing financial support to the Al-Nusra Front, but he was released under pressure from his government, which claimed diplomatic immunity. He was previously a member of the emirate's Olympic Committee, a post to which he was appointed by the Emir himself.

It is more than ever evident that Qatar's princely circle is teeming with Islamist personalities who work on the fringes of terrorism. But the orgy of names is not over, as many other individuals and groups close to the royal family have made it their duty to support the jihadist "resistance" in Syria. Among them: Salim Hasan Khalifa Rashid al-Kuwari, who was—and is likely still—employed by the Qatari government despite being on the U.S. list of sponsors of terrorism. Intelligence documents showed that Al-Kuwari provided material support and hundreds of thousands of dollars to Al-Qaeda facilitators in Iran. He was questioned and detained twice by the Qatari authorities, after which he went back to his former job in the Ministry of Interior as if nothing had happened. Another one, Hamid bin Abdallah al-Ali, also supported the Al-Nusra Front in Syria. In a passionate sermon he delivered at the State Grand Mosque in Doha on March 2, 2012, al-Ali urged the faithful to stand up for the "great jihad." His presence at the Grand Mosque would perhaps have gone unnoticed were it not for the fact that he had been invited by the Ministry of Endowments and Islamic Affairs. One of al-Ali's stooges, Abd al-Latif bin Abdallah Salih Muhammad al-Kawari, has been gravitating around Al-Qaeda's orbit since the 2000s. Kawari was, among other things, involved in the supervision of the Qatar-based fundraising campaign Madid Ahl al-Sham, for the benefit of Al-Qaeda in Syria.

It is now time to talk about Hamas, a jihadist organization that has a strong affinity with the Qatari government. The relations between the kingdom and Hamas date back to around 2008 when Doha had provided the organization with $250 million during the Gaza war (2008-2009). In 2012, the ex-Emir of Qatar, Hamad bin Khalifa al-Thani, had transferred an additional 400 million into the coffers of Hamas to finance the construction of roads and residential complexes in Palestine. In July 2016, the Qatari government came to the rescue of public sector workers in Gaza, an area under Hamas's control, handing out $30 million to help pay their wages. One of the leaders of the jihadist organization, Ismail Haniyeh, had once declared, without any hesitation, that the donations from Qatar would also serve to pay the salaries of its military personnel. Another leader of Hamas, Khaled Meshaal, established his residence in Qatar until June 2017, when he had to leave the country following outside pressure exerted on the Qatari royal family. When addressing the issue of the relations between Hamas and Qatar, we must not fail to mention the organization behind the creation of the Palestinian terrorist group, the Muslim Brotherhood, which also cashes in on Doha's largesse. Here, the financial support granted to the brotherhood is more than significant. One can wonder if its highest dignitaries did not become rich overnight thanks to the generosity of the Gulf emirate. The royal family shelled out no less than $7.5 billion to the Muslim Brotherhood during the short period of Mohammed Morsi's mandate as President of Egypt, that is, between June 2012 and July 2013. Those funds were matched with a media campaign aimed at polishing the image of that government, a pure product of the brotherhood. A campaign that was actually led by Al-Jazeera, a state-owned media that had been very loyal to the Brothers during the Arab Spring, to such an extent that 22 Egyptian employees of the television network had resigned in protest against its bias. No wonder that Qatar is home to one of the most important spiritual leaders of the Muslim Brotherhood: Yusuf al-Qaradawi. Director of a research center at Qatar University, Yusuf al-Qaradawi is a major intellectual influence within the fundamentalist movement of Islam. His extremist positions are legion: 1) he asserts that wife-beating must be permissible after the failure of all other means of persuasion; 2) he refuses to condemn the female genital mutilation; 3) he justifies the murder of homosexuals; 4) he encourages the formation of Muslim ghettos in the West in a project of conquest; 5) he approves of the use of suicide bombers in Israel and claims, as such, that Hitler was sent by Allah to punish the Jews.

Concerned about the poor brand image that it maintains in the West in general and in the United States in particular, Qatar relies on a clique of lobbyists to convince the Western political class that it has nothing to do with terrorism. At the forefront of the emirate's guardian angels features the Brookings Institution, a liberal think tank that hit the jackpot with contracts valued at $14.8 million with the Qatari government for the year 2013 alone. The partnership between this institution and Qatar began in 2002 when the latter started to subsidize the think-tank's outreach program to the Muslim world. A program focused on political correctness that could only attract the attention of a country acting within the confines of radical Islamism. Saleem Ali, formerly a visiting fellow at the Brookings Doha Centre, was being very outspoken when he said to *The New York Times* that it was forbidden to criticize the Qatari government within the Brookings, something he was made aware of during his job interview. The allegation was denied by the think tank but confirmed by none other than Qatar's Ministry of Foreign Affairs. When we closely look at the tedious statements of some prominent members of the Brookings Institution, we have every reason to believe that Saleem Ali was right. In a 2012 report entitled "The Qatari Spring: Qatar's Emerging Role in Peacemaking", Sultan Barakat, research director at the Brookings Doha Center, had described Qatar as an emerging peacemaker and a force for good in the Muslim world. "[D]uring the Arab Spring, Qatar has emerged as a 'reformer'; that is, as a vocal and progressive leader of modern Arab nations, with the willingness and the capacity to utilize a broad range of both hard—and soft—power initiatives to achieve its foreign policy goals", wrote Barakat. Needless to say, only the Brookings Institution could see in Qatar's involvement in Syria a drive to promote peace. In a January 2014 article in *Foreign Policy* magazine, Will McCants, Michael Scott Doran and Clint Watts, foreign policy experts at the Brookings, urged the Obama administration against classifying Ahrar al-Sham as a terrorist organization. Nobody is dumb enough not to see the shadow of the Qatari government behind this move. Another researcher at the Brookings, Ahmet T. Kuru, wrote, in an article published in February 2013, that Recep Tayyip Erdogan's Turkey, a great ally of Qatar in the Syrian conflict, embodied a kind of American secularism, where religion is separated from the state. With the utmost seriousness, Kuru added that Erdogan's party was a "model of governance" for Muslims throughout the Middle East, demonstrating the possibility of "pursuing Muslim politics without establishing an Islamic state."

Turkey's Double Game

Erdogan's Turkey a model of governance for Muslims? "ISIS is a reality and we have to accept that we cannot eradicate a well-organized and popular establishment such as the Islamic State; therefore, I urge my western colleagues to revise their mindset about Islamic political currents, put aside their cynical mentality and thwart Vladimir Putin's plans to crush Syrian Islamist revolutionaries." These comments were made by Hakan Fidan, the head of the Turkish National Intelligence Organization (MIT) and Recep Tayyip Erdogan's most loyal ally. Fidan had had the nerve to add that in order to deal with the large number of foreign jihadists wishing to go to Syria, the Islamic State needed to establish a political office, if not a consulate, in Istanbul. That is just about what the group did. According to the German network *ZDF*, ISIS ran recruitment offices in Turkey, possibly in Istanbul and Gaziantep, from where the future jihadists, for a $4,000 fee, were transferred to Iraq or Syria. Another German media outlet, *ARD*, reported that ISIS had opened another office in the Gaziantep area, this one to ensure the "proper organizing" of the Yazidi slave market. The terrorist organization apparently used WhatsApp and

Telegram apps to sell its sex slaves. Had these offices obtained Ankara's approval?

A freakish fella, this Hakan Fidan. In December 2014, his intelligence service, the MIT, set up camps in Turkey, mostly in the province of Hatay, to muster illegal migrants and train them before they get transferred to Syria. One of those camps, located in the Bayir-Bucak region of northern Syria, was used by the Sultan Abdulhamid Khan Brigade, under the umbrella of the MIT. The brigade was born from the merger of three radical groups, namely Osman Gazi, Omer bin Abdulaziz, and Omer Mukhtar. In Syria, its activities were coordinated with those of the Al-Nusra Front in the governorate of Latakia. The MIT also oversaw the transfer of a large contingent of ISIS fighters, led by the Libyan Mahdi al-Harati, from Libya to Syria. In these maneuvers, one of the organizations that offered the MIT its resources to transport weapons and rebels to Syria is the IHH İnsani Yardim Vakfi, or Foundation for Human Rights and Freedoms and Humanitarian Relief. For those who know absolutely nothing about the IHH, here are some facts you will surely find interesting. The organization was at the heart of what was called the "Gaza flotilla raid", an operation conducted on May 31, 2010, by the Israeli Army against six civilian ships of the flotilla in the Mediterranean Sea. Three of those ships, operated by the Free Gaza Movement and the IHH, were carrying humanitarian aid and construction materials intending to break the Israeli blockade of the Gaza Strip. Israel had warned the leaders of the flotilla to abort their mission, to no avail. The raid had been condemned by the international community, which was ignoring, or pretending to ignore, the terrorist links of the Turkish NGO, links that have been bolstered in Syria. For instance: on September 15, 2014, the IHH transported arms and medical supplies to ISIS from Bursa, Turkey, to Syria via the Ceylanpinar border crossing. The convoy was escorted by the MIT. On September 21, 2015, in Tall Rifaat, Syria, representatives of the Syrian opposition who had received military training in a camp located in Kirsehir, Turkey, had delivered weapons from the port of Iskenderun to the Al-Nusra Front in Idlib, using vehicles provided by the IHH with, as always, the MIT not too far behind as a "protector." This business relationship between the IHH and the Turkish intelligence service is not surprising since the NGO is a major partner of the Turkish Cooperation and Development Agency (TIKA), of which none other than Hakan Fidan was president from 2003 to 2007. According to Ahmet Yayla, a former director of the anti-terrorist section of the Turkish national police in Sanliurfa, Fidan was the No. 1 suspect in attacks committed against leftist intellectuals in the 1990s. The police had tracked down a cell belonging to the Turkish Hezbollah (no affiliation with the Lebanese Hezbollah), an organization listed as a terrorist entity by the American State Department and of which Fidan was a member. The Turkish Hezbollah is little known in the West, but one of its founding members was Haci Bayancuk, whose son, Halis, was until recently the emir of the Islamic State in Turkey.

The IHH, in its warlike adventures, spreads its tentacles far and wide to take advantage of all the influential groups that encompass its ideological universe, which includes Al-Qaeda. In 1997, a police search carried out in the NGO's premises in Istanbul resulted in the discovery of weapons and explosives, as well as evidence of its links to terrorist organizations. Links that have never been severed: in January 2014, the IHH was accused by a prosecutor from the province of Van, in eastern Turkey, of association with Al-Qaeda-affiliated groups. The investigation had led to the IHH when wiretapping showed that the NGO had sent funds, medical supplies and material of all kinds to jihadists. Fearing that the investigators would trace the IHH channels back to the government, Ankara had ordered the stay of proceedings and the arrest of all the police officers and prosecutors involved in the case. The territory of the IHH extends up to the very ends of North Africa, where it interfered in the civil war during the Arab Spring by arming Libyan factions. The intelligence on these operations was obtained from electronic communications involving one of President Erdogan's sons-in-law. It was learned in these communications that the owner of a bankrupt company was seeking compensation from the Erdogan government for the damage suffered by his ship during arms transport to Libyan ports at the express request of the Turkish authorities, in 2011. The communications also revealed all the details of a weapons shipment intended for the rebels and approved by the Turkish government in a ship under contract with none other than the IHH.

Back to Hakan Fidan. The man is quite talkative and does not mince words. Puffed up with arrogance, he takes pride in pleading the cause of his fellows, "eminent" members of the international Islamist circle. Few reacted in the West when the head of the MIT said that it was Turkey's duty to provide medical care to all the wounded fleeing the Russian airstrikes, regardless of their political or religious affiliation. This position was symptomatic of a willingness among the Turks to find another way to act as a sort of fulcrum for the jihadists. As evidence, one of the top Islamic State's commanders, Ahmet el-H. (his full name has never been released), was treated in a Sanliurfa hospital with other activists, at the expense of the Turkish taxpayers. Ahmet Yayla, the terrorism expert we have cited before, revealed that the governor of Sanliurfa had instructed the police to provide 24-hour protection to Islamic State combatants who were being treated in the region's hospitals. Among these combatants was another ISIS commander, Fadel Ahmad Abdullah al-Hiyali (a.k.a. Abu Muslim al-Turkmani). And at least one more known fighter from the jihadist group, who had been injured in Kobane (Syria), was admitted to a hospital in the province of Denizli. But ISIS men were not the only ones to receive medical assistance in Turkey. In July 2013, an Al-Nusra Front commander was treated in a hospital in Ceylanpinar, near the Syrian border. Other wounded from the same group had preceded or followed him, so much so that the locals had complained to the *Hurriyet* newspaper that there was no room left for them in any medical facility. A fighter from Ahrar al-Sham was also admitted to a hospital in Antakya, where he died, and several from the Islamic Front, mostly made up of Islamists, were treated in Gaziantep. Mohammed al-Zahawi, the former head of the Ansar al-Sharia group, in part responsible for the attack on the American diplomatic mission in Benghazi, Libya, also died in a Turkish hospital where he had been treated for an injury sustained in a battle. Turkey went so far as to repatriate his body to Misrata, Libya, for the funeral.

That phenomenon provided a golden opportunity to do business. In a November 24, 2014, telephone call intercepted by the Turkish authorities, an Islamic State smuggler, Ilhami Bali, was speaking with the owner of a consultancy firm called M.I.S Danismanlik, which was acting as an intermediary in the transport of wounded jihadists to Turkish hospitals. The two men were discussing financial arrangements for the cost of the medical care needed for 16 ISIS militants, which amounted to $62,000. In another conversation, the same consultant complained about unpaid bills amounting to $150,000 for surgeries performed on ISIS militants. It is even said, sarcastically, that the demand for medical care was greater than the supply of services, which led to a proliferation of makeshift hospitals in the Turkish territory. Journalist and documentary maker Tuluhan Tekelioglu reported in November 2013 that at least four of those makeshift hospitals were funded by Saudi Arabian non-governmental organizations. Tekelioglu was never able to prove that the Turkish government was aware of the existence of those facilities, but one thing is sure, "the transfers of wounded [were] part of the war economy", she said, adding that smugglers were carrying "wounded fighters across the border every day." The situation was such that a nurse from the coastal town of Mersin, in the south of the country, wrote a letter to the authorities, saying that she was fed up with looking after the members of the Islamic State. "We treat them, then they kidnap people […]", she wrote. "Many […] activists have come here for treatment. They just returned to battle after they left." The care provided to Syrian jihadists in Turkey was not a precedent, though. A Hamas official, Imad al-Alami, underwent surgery in a Turkish hospital, long before the Syrian crisis. Those privileges granted to jihadists in Turkish health facilities lasted until 2015, when President Obama asked his counterpart, Recep Tayyip Erdogan, to put an end to this practice.

Ilhami Bali, the head of M.I.S Danismanlik, was a major smuggler for the Islamic State, but not only: he was also one of the major players in a deadly attack committed in the Turkish capital, Ankara, on October 10, 2015, killing 109 people. Bali and other ISIS activists had targeted NGOs as well as supporters of leftist and pro-Kurdish parties who were organizing a peace rally outside the city's main train station.

Before the attack, no fewer than 62 intelligence reports had gathered enough information to foresee an all ISIS disaster. On September 14, 2015, the anti-terrorist wing of the Turkish police sent an "intelligence alert" about an ISIS team training in a camp in Deir ez-Zor, a city in eastern Syria. The information relating to the alert noted that the ISIS team's mission consisted in organizing a large-scale suicide attack targeting a meeting in Turkey and in hijacking a ship or a plane full of passengers. Both the investigation and the trial that followed showed that the Erdogan government, willing to hide the evidence of links between its security forces and Ilhami Bali, did everything to remove information, obstruct the work of investigators and turn down any request submitted by the lawyers representing the victims of the attack and their families. These have not been more successful before the Constitutional Court that dismissed their complaints, contending that the government had not violated their fundamental rights in limiting access to the prosecution's files. At least two other recordings of telephone conversations proved that Ilhami Bali was the right man within ISIS for everything associated with the smuggling of jihadists. In one of those recordings, we can hear a Georgian by the name of Lasha Nadirashvili confirming to Bali that four recruits were waiting to be fetched from a shopping center in Gaziantep, a city located an hour's drive from Turkey's southern border. In another conversation dated November 20, 2014, a Russian, Oleksandr Pushchuk, was planning with Bali the future crossing of eleven recruits into Syria. Investigation records show that ISIS, in some cases, used gas stations, mosques, and even a soccer field as meeting places for recruits to avoid their being identified. On average, the terrorist group could smuggle, in its best moments, from 50 to more than 100 militants across the Turkish-Syrian border every day. For instance, between October 17 and November 18, 2014, 1,440 militants crossed the border through the sole Bali network. Wiretapping reveals that 469 other militants did the same between November 18 and 25. These figures reflect cross-border traffic generated exclusively in the district of Elbeyli, in the province of Kilis. The Turkish police, it should be noted, was spying on Bali, but the smuggler has never had to pay the price for its links to the Islamic State. During a surveillance operation in Gaziantep from June 4 to November

4, 2014, the police intercepted and recorded 997 telephone conversations between ISIS suspects, including Bali. In a conversation dated September 5, 2014, a Turkish soldier can be heard addressing the chief smuggler, calling him "sheikh" out of deference. The two men agreed that neither side should strike the other, and Bali had confirmed to the soldier that his organization had issued an order to instruct its militants to avoid harming Turkish men in uniform. Investigation records also show that ISIS hired lawyers to release foreign recruits detained by the Turkish police, a move that generally resulted in instant success.

The relations between jihadists and Recep Tayyip Erdogan's Islamized Turkey were discovered very early on by an American journalist, Serena Shim. Shim had reported some troubling facts before dying in a car accident in October 2014. As early as 2012, she began a series of TV reports in which recruits for the Syrian jihad were seen crossing the Turkish border with impunity to join the Islamic State in what appeared to be refugee camps. The journalist had revealed that the recruits were taken by truck up to the Syrian border and that shipments of arms were diverted to jihadists via the Incirlik U.S. Air Base in Turkey. The refugee camps were, in fact, nothing more than training grounds watched over by Turkish soldiers. According to Serena Shim, some of the trucks carrying the future jihadists belonged to an organization called the World Food Organization. Was it rather the UN World Food Program? At the time, Shim was one of the few reporters to witness those events. Even today, many people, starting with members of her family, believe that her car accident was the result of a deliberate act and that she was the victim of an assassination. In one of her last reports, Shim said that she feared for her life, just after being accused of spying by the MIT. Whether or not she was the victim of a criminal act, Serena Shim was right: Turkey helped the Islamic State and other jihadist groups recruit fighters for their military campaigns in Syria. And this support to the die-hard jihadists was "courtesy" of none other than Hakan Fidan's MIT. An MIT that was, on top of that, directly involved in arms trafficking. We have seen in previous pages that the intelligence service was connected to the Foundation for Human Rights and Freedoms and Humanitarian Relief in, among other things, the transport of weapons.

But it was not the only time Hakan Fidan's organization was involved in such a scheme. On at least two occasions, in November 2013 and January 2014, men from the national police intercepted trucks loaded with weapons that were heading toward the Turkish-Syrian border from the Adana province. The first convoy, that of November 2013, had been successfully seized, but the convoy of January 2014, which comprised three vehicles, continued on its way under threats made against the police by MIT officers. In public, President Erdogan claimed that the trucks were carrying medical supplies, but nothing could be further from the truth. The vehicles were loaded with six containers, mostly filled with portable missiles and ammunition. And since everything is going wrong nowadays in Turkey, Ozcan Sisman and Aziz Takci, the two magistrates who had ordered the search of the vehicles, were detained upon the application of state prosecutors, willing accomplices of the Erdogan government. As for the truck seized in November 2013, it contained pieces of mortar. The search warrant, in that case, had referred to a police investigation that had discovered that the pieces of mortar were to be shipped to a training camp used by Al-Qaeda on the Syrian border. The truck driver had confessed to carrying the cargo down to Reyhanli, under the protection of the MIT. The Turkish population was unaware of those stories until May 29, 2015, when the *Cumhuriyet* newspaper published photos and videos showing one of the convoys carrying weapons. The problem is that in Turkey, telling the truth can have dramatic consequences: in July 2015, four prosecutors and a local gendarmerie commander were arrested and charged with attempting to "overthrow the government through violence and coercion" in relation to the events described above. Then, in November 2015, an Istanbul court subservient to the Erdogan government indicted Can Dundar, *Cumhuriyet*'s editor-in-chief, and Erdem Gul, the paper's Ankara bureau chief, for spying and "divulging state secrets." Another Turkish newspaper, *Bugün*, was raided after it reported the transfer of weapons and explosives to ISIS operatives from Turkey. Yet, all this information had been confirmed by the Islamic State itself. Savas Yildiz, one of the organization's fighters who were captured by Kurdish forces, revealed that troops were moving freely in Turkish territory under the aegis of the MIT. At one point, border outposts were dismantled during specific hours to allow groups of 20 to 30 ISIS fighters to pass through, unhindered and undetected. The Turkish military even opened lines of communication with the jihadist organization after it invaded Mosul, Iraq, in June 2014.

Despite Turkey's wrongdoing, an Erdogan government's official had boasted that his country was not too soft with ISIS and that it was taking all the necessary measures to address the national threat posed by the terrorist group. That was certainly not the opinion of the family of Ahmet Beyaztas, a car mechanic of Kurdish origin. At home in the dull industrial city of Dilovasi, "a polluted and poverty-stricken community on the fringe of Istanbul", as described by *Newsweek*, Ahmet Beyaztas's brother, Kenan, told reporters how local ISIS supporters openly displayed the organization's banner on the windows of their cars and homes without being disturbed by law enforcement agencies. Young men often boarded minibuses heading to Syria to join ISIS fighters. Ahmet Beyaztas was one of those young men. Many accounts of Turkish border guards accepting bribes in exchange for a free pass have also been detailed. Trucks loaded with parts used to manufacture bombs could easily drive through the customs, according to an ISIS defector. Documents seized in ISIS premises show that fighters from around the world were crossing the Turkish-Syrian border with impunity to join their troops in Syria. Several of them were landing at the Adana and Istanbul airports and had permission from the Turkish government to stay in Turkey before heading to Syria. The documents included Turkish passports, transport tickets, residence permits and other materials from the Ministry of Immigration. It was learned in this matter that Syrian passports discovered near the bodies of two of the November 2015 Paris attackers were fake; many think they had likely been forged in Turkey. A Turkish daily newspaper that cited a Uighur source reported that 100,000 Turkish passports were forged on behalf of the Islamic State, an exaggerated figure according to the U.S. Army's Foreign Studies Military Office (FSMO) but confirmed by *Sky News Arabia*, which mentioned that the Turkish government itself approved the passports of foreign militants crossing the Turkey-Syria border to gain access to ISIS camps. The passports bore the official exit stamp of the Turkish border control, which is quite disturbing as investigators from the European Union (Europol) found fake passports in refugee camps in Greece. In this regard, the Italian newspaper *La Stampa* revealed that ISIS had attempted to infiltrate refugee groups in Europe. This issue had previously been raised by Jordan's Minister of Foreign Affairs, Nasser Judeh, during a meeting with American officials. Because the Russian bombings had prevented Turkey from establishing safe zones to stop the flow of Syrian refugees, the Turkish government "unleashed [them] onto Europe", Judeh had said.

It is true that Turkey's neighboring countries, with the exception of Iran and Qatar, were not happy about the Erdogan government's close relations with the jihadists. In October 2014, an Egyptian official publicly denounced the Turkish services for giving satellite photos and general information to the Islamic State. On January 11, 2016, King Abdullah of Jordan, as his Minister of Foreign Affairs had done before, alluded to the ties between Turkey and ISIS during a meeting with representatives of the United States Congress. The king had stated that the refugee crisis in Europe and the presence of terrorists in his own country were not an accident of history, pointing out that the Turkish government was encouraging ISIS to send militants to Europe to carry out terrorist attacks and that it was assisting the jihadist group in the Iraqi and Syrian oil trade. Abdullah had also said that Ankara was supporting Islamist groups not only in Syria but also in Libya and Somalia. The king's remarks were not a distortion of facts, as we have seen, especially his accusations concerning the illegal trading in oil. The Russians, in this respect, published images showing long lineups of tankers at the Turkish border around Zakho, in Iraqi Kurdistan. The presence of these vehicles was likely authorized by the Erdogan government. At one point, between 100 and 150 tankers were passing through Turkish checkpoints every day. ISIS's oil supply chain covered a long territory, including the Turkish cities of Sanliurfa, Siirt, Batman, Osmaniye, Gaziantep, Sirnak, Adana, Kahramanmaras, Adiyaman, and Mardin. Here again, the border guards played an important role in facilitating the passage of the deliveries in exchange for bribes. ISIS, at the height of its glory, reportedly managed to collect daily a million dollars from the oil trade. On a normal day, an oil trafficker could reap about $1,500, of which $500 landed in the pockets of intermediaries on the Syrian side, and $500 were given out to the border guards. In Turkey, the oil was delivered, among other places, to a Tüpras (Turkish Petroleum Refineries Co.) refinery located in Batman, just over 900 miles southeast of Ankara. Most of the hydrocarbon stocks were therefore shipped to the Mediterranean coast from Turkish terminals, mainly through the port of Ceyhan. Among the companies involved in the resale of oil extracted under ISIS control were Palmali Shipping (Turkey), General Energy (UK and Turkey), and Saudi Aramco (Saudi Arabia). Palmali Shipping belonged to the Azerbaijani billionaire Mübariz Mansimov, a very good acquaintance of the Turkish President Recep Tayyip Erdogan. A dictator-like President, but above all, an authentic crook. The Erdogan family owns an oil tanker worth $25 million called Agdash, and the deal that allowed the Erdogans to acquire the ship was concluded with the help of Mübariz Mansimov and another close friend of the President, Sitki Ayan. It was a very profitable deal for the clan as it never had to pay one cent for the purchase of the ship. Everything went through a series of suspicious fund movements from offshore companies based in Malta and the Isle of Man, with Mübariz Mansimov at the forefront. This obscure oligarch, in reality, donated the ship to the President, which proved to be a good idea because his business boomed in Turkey, thanks in part to the help he received from the Turkish government. Beginning as a mere maritime entrepreneur, the billionaire became a heavyweight in the fields of health, energy, buildings and public works, tourism, air transport, and luxury cars. He was notably offered to develop a prestigious port station in the city of Bodrum, in the southwest of the Mediterranean. This station is called the "billionaires club" as it attracted celebrities and aristocrats such as Prince Charles and Bill Gates. In his best period, Mansimov owned almost 100 freighters and his empire controlled about two thirds of the oil trade in the Black Sea region. All good things come to an end, though, as in May 2018, Palmali LLC was officially declared bankrupt.

Syria's Double Game

Bashar al-Assad was caught off-guard during the first quarter of 2011. It is as if he had never foreseen the wave of the Arab Spring that would sweep through his country. Libya, Yemen, Tunisia saw their governments fall one after another, but al-Assad probably thought that Syria was to escape such a fate. Yet, it was easy to predict that this country would not be spared by the wind of freedom that was blowing at the time in the Arab world. A wind of freedom perhaps more akin to a wind of Salafism, though, and in this regard, the Syrian President was lucid enough to understand that he was the one, at the outset, who had allowed the "Salafist-jihadists" to turn up in his backyard. To better understand the logic behind this story, we must go back to 2003 when the presidential palace was gripped by panic after the rapid victory of the American forces over Saddam Hussein's troops. After Iraq, it was speculated in Damascus, President Bush was surely willing to walk on Syria's turf. In the Syrian intelligence backrooms, it was decided to arrange for the transfer to Iraq of thousands of radical fighters mostly coming from Libya, Saudi Arabia and Tunisia to swell the ranks of Al-Qaeda and thus throw a spanner in the works of the Americans. Ninety percent of the jihadists who fought in Iraq entered via the Syrian route. In the first eleven days after the overthrow of Saddam Hussein, just under 5,000 foreign fighters had left the Syrian territory to go to Iraq. On the twelfth day, more than 1,000 Syro-Palestinians were added to this list. In June 2005, the *Guardian* had devoted an article to this issue: "Each neighborhood [of Aleppo] started sending buses loaded with mujahideen into Iraq", the newspaper's source, a resident of Aleppo called Abu Ibrahim, had said. The call to jihad was openly encouraged by the Syrian government, according to Abu Ibrahim, and several buses crossing the border were precisely chartered by the regime. Damascus even cut the price of passport fees. Simply put, everything was in place to make the crossing easy. Meanwhile, recalled *The Guardian*, "the Syrian media were banging the drum for jihad." Eyewitnesses said that the Syrian border police "were waving to the jihadi buses as they crossed into Iraq." The government, although secular, had allowed the ex-Grand Mufti of Syria, Ahmad Kuftaro, a man known for his religious tolerance, to issue a fatwa legitimizing suicide attacks. The whole of Syria had thus gathered around the "freedom fighters." At the same time, Iraqi Baathists loyal to Saddam Hussein fled in the opposite direction, finding refuge in Syria to establish their new regional command, where they could raise funds, collect weapons and train staff for the insurgency. Intelligence reports mentioned that Al-Qaeda in Iraq had convened at least one meeting on Syrian territory, probably with the knowledge of the al-Assad government. At the end of 2004, Washington, which was piling up dead bodies in Iraq, began to put pressure on Damascus to crack down on Baathists and jihadists. In response, al-Assad feigned to comply with the requirements by arresting hundreds of insurgents. The arrests made headlines, but Syria quietly released the vast majority of those insurgents in the days following their arrest. It was just a rehearsal of what would occur in 2011 when the regime would release a large proportion of those who would become commanders in jihadist groups. This was the case of Hassan Aboud, member of the Ahrar al-Sham group, and Zahran Alloush, of Jaysh al-Islam, both detained in Syrian prisons before the Arab Spring. When these organizations were still in an embryonic state in Syria, al-Assad did not budge an inch, leaving them some time to boost their workforce. In doing so, the Syrian president wanted the world to see how the opposition was packed with shady Islamists.

In early 2005, al-Assad was put under increased international pressure as new evidence linked his regime to the assassination of former Lebanese Prime Minister Rafic Hariri on February 14. This international pressure was likely behind the dictator's decision to turn over 30 Baathist leaders, including Saddam's half-brother, Sabawi Ibrahim al-Tikriti, to Iraq. In May 2005, the Syrian Ambassador to the United States, Imad Moustapha, claimed that his government had arrested approximately 1,200 foreign fighters who were heading to the Iraqi border. It was, however, too little too late. In an ironic twist of fate, these radicals would change sides in 2011 and attempt to bring down the very one who had allowed them to come forward in Iraq. This was a strange combination of circumstances, but it was without counting on al-Assad's political shrewdness. When the

President/dictator became aware that Islamic State troops were each day gaining control of large swathes of Syrian territory while fighting the Free Syrian Army, he decided that it was time to seal an alliance with the devil. In 2014, the Syrian Air Force fighters began bombing rebel positions to allow ISIS to make strategic gains. In return, the emir of ISIS, Abu Bakr al-Baghdadi, forbade his men from shooting at Syrian forces on the ground. A survey by Jane's Terrorism and Insurgency Center found that, from January 1 to November 21, 2014, only 6% of the attacks carried out by the Syrian government forces had been directed against ISIS, while during the same period, 13% of this group's attacks had targeted Damascus's troops. At this time, Syria was even buying oil directly from the jihadist group. For that matter, a European Union report dated March 2015 drew attention to the relationship between the Syrian regime and ISIS in this field. Both, it is written in the report, jointly operated a HESCO gas plant in Al-Thawrah, in central Syria. The plant was supplying, among other facilities, the power plants run by the regime. In addition, on June 28, 2015, a source close to the Turkish intelligence services had pointed out that an agreement had been concluded between Damascus and ISIS to "destroy" the Free Syrian Army (FSA) in the northern parts of the country. According to this source, a group of commanders from both sides had met on May 28, 2015, in a gas production plant in northeastern Syria's Al-Shaddadah region to make up a plan of attack against the FSA rebels. This is a curious paradox since, as we have seen, the Islamic State partnered with the FSA in certain occasions. But the fact is this arrangement between the regime and ISIS left many foreign fighters, those who had imagined the jihad differently, deeply disillusioned. Their disenchantment was short-lived, though, as al-Baghdadi's troops quickly made a U-turn to attack their "protector." The question remains whether al-Assad, knowing that the Americans were seeking to destabilize his regime, had no choice but to make some concessions to the jihadists. Perhaps he considered that the U.S. government had been too ungrateful after all the services that Syria had rendered to its country in the aftermath of 9/11.

To Hell With the Law

It was the time of the "extraordinary renditions", a program conducted by the CIA and whose purpose was to operate outside the judicial framework, an approach the agency has used on many occasions since its inception. The extraordinary renditions were not created by the hawks of the Bush administration, but they squeezed it until there was not a single drop left, to put it bluntly. Following the September 11 attacks, the program became one of the mainstays of Washington's war on terror. This was when President Bush issued a directive allowing the CIA to perform these extraordinary renditions without prior authorization from the White House, the Justice Department, or the State Department. A process he renewed on July 20, 2007, when he issued another directive this time to allow the continuation of the program. This measure flouted the *Policy With Respect to the Involuntary Return of Persons in Danger of Subjection to Torture*, implemented in 1998, which states the following: "It shall be the policy of the United States not to expel, extradite, or otherwise effect the involuntary return of any person to a country in which there are substantial grounds for believing the person would be in danger of being subjected to torture, regardless of whether the person is physically present in the United States." Scott Horton, an international law expert who helped prepare a report on extraordinary renditions on behalf of the New York University School of Law and the New York City Bar Association, believes that about 150 individuals were "brought to justice" from 2001 to 2005 as part of the CIA-led program. Although "brought to justice" is a somewhat twisted formula in the circumstances. The Open Society Foundations, on its side, identified 136 cases involving extraordinary renditions under the Bush administration; 54 foreign governments are said to have participated in those operations in various ways, in particular, 1) by accepting that the CIA set up secret prisons ("black sites") on their territory, 2) by using torture to interrogate the individuals subjected to these renditions, 3) by assisting in the capture and transfer of detainees, 4) by allowing the use of domestic airspace and airports for secret flights transporting the said detainees, or 5) by providing intelligence leading to the secret detention and extraordinary rendition.

Chilling stories abound. We only need a few examples to see the extent of the damage caused by the CIA program. On October 21, 2001, Hadj Boudella, a Muslim of Algerian extraction, and five other Algerians living in Bosnia were arrested after the American authorities tipped off the Bosnian government about a so-called conspiracy to blow up the British and American Embassies in Sarajevo. One of the suspects had supposedly made about 70 phone calls to Abu Zubaydah, an Al-Qaeda official, a few days after 9/11. The problem is that Boudella claimed that neither he nor his pals knew the man who allegedly contacted Zubaydah. What is more, the Bosnian government's investigation failed to trace the famous calls made to Zubaydah. Regardless of these failures, the same government detained the six men for three months at the request of the United States, which has never been able to prove that they had committed any crime. On January 17, 2002, a judgment from the Supreme Court of Bosnia ordered their release, but the defendants' troubles were far from over. Right out of jail, "they were handcuffed, forced to put on surgical masks with nose clips, covered in hoods, and herded into [...] unmarked cars by masked men, some of whom appeared to be members of the Bosnian special forces", reported *The New Yorker*. Six days after this apparent abduction, Boudella and his "accomplices" were transferred to Guantanamo. One of them said that American soldiers broke two of his fingers. Boudella was finally released on December 16, 2008, and was able to return to Bosnia. He has never been formally charged in court.

On December 18, 2001, at Stockholm's Bromma Airport, security officials took Mohammed al-Zery and Ahmed Agiza, two Egyptian asylum seekers, to an empty office, where they forcibly administered sedatives to them using a suppository and instructed them to slip on an orange jumpsuit. Blindfolded, handcuffed and legs shackled, the suspects were then transported to Cairo on a United States-registered Gulfstream aircraft. The Swedish authorities claimed with almost childish naivety that they had received assurances from the Egyptians that al-Zery and Agiza would be treated humanely, but that was, of course, a lie. Both men said through their lawyers and family members that they were tortured with electrical charges inflicted on the genitals. Al-Zery was ultimately released after spending two years in an Egyptian prison. Agiza, who used to be an ally of the current head of Al-Qaeda, Ayman al-Zawahiri, but who has apparently renounced violence, was convicted of terrorism by Egypt's Supreme Military Court and sentenced to twenty-five years in prison.

In April 2011, the *Associated Press* reported that suspected terrorists had been secretly detained and interrogated in Afghanistan in twenty temporary sites. Only in 2010, more than a dozen individuals were held for several weeks at the Bagram Air Base, run by the U.S. Joint Operations Special Command (JSOC). They were forced to strip naked and kept in solitary confinement in windowless cells round the clock. A report from the Open Society Foundations, based on interviews with more than 20 former JSOC detainees in Bagram, confirmed these facts. Besides Bagram, another site was called "Dark Prison", where men were held in total darkness. Documents also referred to a site called "Salt Pit", located in an abandoned brick factory, and rumors spread about three other secret CIA prisons in Afghanistan: one sat in the Panjshir Valley, while nothing is known about the location of the other two, identified as "Rissat 1" and "Rissat 2." Apart from hosting those secret prisons, Afghanistan also authorized the use of its airports and airspace for flights reportedly connected to the extraordinary renditions program. Court records show that at least thirteen flights operated by Richmor Aviation, a company involved in the transportation of CIA victims, landed in Afghanistan. Richmor was, in fact, a subcontractor for Sportsflight, a Long Island aircraft brokerage firm. The business relationship between the two companies did not last, though, as Richmor eventually sued Sportsflight for breach of contract. "In the process", wrote *The Washington Post*, "the costs and itineraries of numerous CIA flights became part of the court record." This is how it was learned that for 36 months between 2002 and 2005, Richmor flew at least 1,258 hours on behalf of the CIA. The American company billed $4,900 an hour, therefore earning revenues of about $6 million over three years, courtesy of Washington and its Langley henchmen. But Richmor only accounted for a small percentage of CIA's business, which suggests that the agency, following the September-11 attacks, shelled out tens of millions of dollars to use private planes for the transportation of not only detainees but also its own staff. Egypt was also active in the extraordinary renditions program, perhaps even more intensely than any other Islamist state. The Egyptian government transferred many individuals in the same way as it authorized the use of its airspace and airports for flights connected to the CIA operations. More importantly, Egypt was described as "the country to which the greatest numbers of rendered suspects have been sent [by the U.S.]." In 2005, the Egyptian Prime Minister himself acknowledged that the United States had transferred 60 to 70 "suspects" to his country.

What may seem odd is that three enemies of America served as emergency channels to its controversial program during this period when the law lost its name. These countries are Iran, Libya, and Syria. In March 2002, the Iranian government transferred fifteen individuals to the Afghan government, which in turn handed ten of them over to the United States. At least six of those individuals were secretly detained by the CIA in Afghanistan. Libya also arrested, interrogated and tortured individuals as part of the extraordinary renditions program, just as it authorized the use of its airspace and airports for the same operations. Documents discovered after the fall of the Gaddafi regime, combined with previous reports, show that the United States transferred at least eleven individuals to Libya for interrogation. But for a while, it is Syria, not Libya, Egypt, or Afghanistan, that found itself at the top of Washington's list of supporters in its counterterrorism campaign. As early as December 2001, American agents had arranged for a German national to be transferred to a Syrian prison and questioned by a unit of the Syrian intelligence services called the "Palestine Branch", known for its use of torture and summary executions. Equipped with a list of questions provided by the Americans, the interrogators managed to obtain answers that "satisfied" the two parties. This German national sent to Syria was Mohammed Haydar Zammar, a businessman suspected by the United States of helping to recruit some of the 9/11 hijackers. Zammar was part of the infamous Al-Qaeda's Hamburg cell, which included the leader of the hijackers, Mohammed Atta. At the request of the United States, the jihadist was arrested in Morocco by local police and then transferred to Damascus. In late 2002, he was one of four men held in the "Palestine Branch" prison in the Syrian capital, thanks to the CIA program. He was released in September 2013 in the course of a prisoner swap between the Ahrar al-Sham rebel group and the Syrian government. A source told *Der Spiegel* newspaper that a few days after his release, Zammar went to the Syrian city of Raqqa to join ISIS. He was allegedly behind transfers of funds made to a militant group called Ansar Bayt al-Maqdis, based in Sinai, Egypt. He was later captured by members of the Kurdish People's Protection Units in March 2018 near Deir ez-Zor and is currently being held in a prison in Qamishli, Northern Syria. Three former prisoners incarcerated in Damascus said that they were regularly beaten by Syrian interrogators and detained in cells barely longer and wider than "coffins."

One of the most well-known cases of extraordinary rendition is that of Maher Arar, a Canadian telecommunications engineer born in Syria who was held into *cell 2* of the prison run by the "Palestine Branch." Arar left Syria at 17 and married a Tunisian student from McGill University in Montreal. In September 2002, while on his way home from a vacation in Tunisia with a Canadian passport, he was arrested at New York's John F. Kennedy Airport by FBI agents who immediately ordered his deportation to his native Syria. He was then transferred to Jordan on a Gulfstream aircraft before being flown to Syria, where he was locked up in the jails of the "Palestine Branch." After days of beatings, Arar felt compelled to write a false statement claiming that he had been trained in a terrorist camp in Afghanistan. "I was ready to accept a 10-, 20-year sentence, and say anything, just to get to another place", he said. He was released after months of captivity in Syria. A few years later, he was exonerated and rehabilitated by the Canadian government, which opened the door for him to legal action against the United States. A New York federal judge, however, dismissed the lawsuit on national security grounds. On January 26, 2007, after months of negotiations between the Canadian government and Arar's legal counsel, Prime Minister Stephen Harper officially apologized to the Syrian and announced that his government would give him $10.5 million as compensation and an additional one million for legal costs.

Sarin Attacks: Bashar al-Assad Was Not the Only Culprit

On April 6, 2017, U.S. President Donald Trump authorized the launching of Tomahawk missiles on the Shayrat Airbase, in central Syria, in response to a "deadly attack" that occurred two days earlier in the rebel city of Khan Shaykhun. The international community, excluding Russia and Iran, had condemned this "chemical attack" carried out, it was said, by the Syrian air force. The gas used, sarin possibly mixed with chlorine, according to the official line, caused the death of 89 civilians and left about 500 injured. On April 11, 2017, the Turkish Minister of Health announced that blood and urine tests taken from wounded treated in Turkish hospitals confirmed the use of sarin, an extremely toxic synthetic organophosphorus compound. The information was corroborated the following day by the United Kingdom, whose conclusions showed that the gas used in the attack was "sarin or a similar nerve agent." The Organization for the Prohibition of Chemical Weapons (OPCW) followed suit on April 19, and seven days later, France published a report that concluded that biomedical examinations of the victims conducted out of samples taken on the spot showed that the neurotoxic gas used in Khan Shaykhun (sarin) came from stocks belonging to the Syrian regime, a proof that the latter had not destroyed them all, as it had promised to do so in 2013. The report went on to mention that the components applied in the synthesis process of the nerve gas had been developed in the laboratories belonging to the state-run Syrian Scientific Studies and Research Center (SSRC). Those components were known to the French thanks to the testimony of scientists who used to work at the SSRC before fleeing Syria at the start of the civil war.

Despite this flood of "evidence", Khan Shaykhun did not witness a chemical attack, according to journalist Seymour Hersh, whose story is based on a source who held senior positions both in the U.S. Defense Department and in the CIA. The narrative that covers the Khan Shaykhun case would be "a fairy tale", said Hersh's source. Trump, therefore, gave the order to bomb the Syrian airbase even though he had been warned by his security services that there was no evidence the Syrians used chemical weapons on April 4, 2017. That day, the Syrian troops, using chemical-free conventional explosives they had obtained from Russia, had struck a jihadist hideout. All the technical data for the attack had been supplied beforehand by the Russians to the American military officials. Russian and Syrian air forces officers had made sure to provide the details of the flight path to and from Khan Shaykhun—in English—"to the deconfliction monitors aboard the AWACS plane, which was on patrol near the Turkish border, 60 miles or more to the north", wrote Hersh. By doing so, the Russians wanted to ensure that any CIA asset or informant who had successfully infiltrated the jihadist ring was forewarned not to approach the target designated at Khan Shaykhun. The target in question was a two-story cinder block building in the north of the city. The Russian intelligence services had discovered that a meeting of Ahrar al-Sham and Al-Nusra Front leaders was to take place in that building that was serving as a command and control center for these two groups. It housed "a grocery and other commercial premises on its ground floor with other essential shops nearby, including a fabric shop and an electronics store", but its basement, on the other hand, was used as a warehouse. This is where rockets, weapons and ammunition were stored, as well as chemicals such as chlorine-based decontaminants that Muslims use to cleanse the bodies of the dead before the burial. The target was struck as planned at 6:55 a.m. on April 4, just before midnight in Washington. The 500-pound Syrian bomb triggered a series of secondary explosions that generated a huge toxic cloud formed by the release of the fertilizers, disinfectants and other chemicals kept in the basement of the building. Four jihadists reportedly died in the attack. At first, Khan Shaykhun's initial report mainly came from the White Helmets, a first responder group known for its close association with the Syrian opposition. Then, a team of Médecins sans frontiers/Doctors Without Borders (MSF) stated that "eight patients [from Khan Shaykhun] showed symptoms—including constricted pupils, muscle spasms and involuntary defecation—which are consistent with exposure to a neurotoxic agent such as sarin gas or similar compounds." The MSF team members visited the hospitals where the victims were treated and found that the latter "smelled of bleach, suggesting that they had been exposed to chlorine." In fact, the evidence gathered in the field proved that more than one chemical was responsible for the symptoms observed in the dead and wounded, which would not have been the case had the Syrian Air Force dropped a sarin bomb, says Seymour Hersh. The symptoms were thus typical of exposure to a mixture of chemicals, including chlorine and organophosphates used in many fertilizers.

During those critical days, President Trump's inner circle was completely delusional. What led to this state of mind was a communication intercepted before the attack by an "allied nation" and in which a Syrian general was heard discussing a "special" weapon. There was no mention of neurotoxic gases or sarin, but it did not matter to Washington's politicos: there needed to be a strong response to the attack so that the world realized once for all that America was still the only military superpower. Yet, Secretary of Defense James Mattis himself acknowledged that there was no evidence that sarin had been used by the regime in Khan Shaykhun. Experts, including Hans Blix, former head of the United Nations Monitoring, Verification and Inspection Commission, also questioned the official rhetoric. Others rightly pointed out that Syria, at the time of the American airstrike, was on the verge of winning the war with the help of the Russians and had no need for use of weapons of mass destruction. But President Trump's wish was to get his hunting trophy: on April 6, 2017, 59 Tomahawk missiles were fired on the Shayrat Airbase, near the city of Homs, from two U.S. Navy destroyers in the Mediterranean. The missiles had a light payload: approximately 220 pounds of HBX, an explosive developed during the Second World War. The airbase's fuel storage tanks were pulverized by the bombing, triggering a huge fire and clouds of smoke visible for miles around. No fewer than 24 missiles missed their targets and only a few Tomahawks made their way into the hangars, destroying nine Syrian aircraft, all of them non-operational, according to Seymour Hersh.

A similar story was also challenged by a report from the Massachusetts Institute of Technology (MIT), for which Bashar al-Assad was not behind the attack on Ghouta that took place in 2013. The difference here is that sarin had been used in that case. Written by Richard Lloyd, a former UN expert on missiles, and MIT Professor Theodore Postol, the report shows that the chemical attacks were launched from an area held by the Syrian rebels and not by the state army. It also mentioned that the rockets had all the characteristics of short-range Grad missiles, on which were fixed barrels of gas. The French newspaper *Le Point*, quoting a researcher, had stressed that the Grad missile is known as a low-end weapon, having a range of 1.2 to 3.1 miles with conventional weapons. The same researcher added that the missile lacks precision, which would explain the high number of civilian losses in the Ghouta chemical attack. Seymour Hersh, who is seen today as a black sheep among the media elite, had also questioned the official narrative concerning the same attack. The massacre had left between several hundred and nearly 2,000 dead, according to various estimates, the vast majority of them civilians. Once again, the investigations had led to charges against the Syrian government. On the front line of the accusers were the United Nations, which, it had pointed out, had accumulated overwhelming evidence confirming the use of sarin gas. That statement had not gone unnoticed in Moscow, which had taken no time to blame the international organization for its "bias" against Syria. And in the media conglomerates, the watchword was to carefully respect the editorial line, as it was well demonstrated by Hélène Sallon of *Le Monde* newspaper, who said that "the Western powers had gathered a body of evidence thanks to the videos filmed by witnesses of the attacks, to doctors' reports, to satellite images, to assessments of various intelligence services and, in particular, to the interception of telephone conversations by Syrian officials." *The Washington Post* went further, reporting that U.S. intelligence had recorded each stage of the chemical attack, whose planning had started on August 18. It was known, for instance, that the Syrian Army had used gas masks and that Syrian officials had undertaken an assessment of the operation right after the attack. Information was gleaned in part through the recording of a message intended for the Syrian teams responsible for carrying out the bombings. The *Post* had been careful to specify that the recording had not been provided to the media in order to protect the sources and methods. This might be seen as a reasonable decision, but it is important to mention that the same process followed by Seymour Hersh had been criticized by his detractors. He too has always wanted to protect his sources by refusing to reveal them, something for which he has been condemned by the media elite. It appears that one journalist's anonymous sources can be deemed less credible than those quoted by others, on the grounds that they do not agree with the main narrative, which is quite disturbing.

Now, if the Goutha and Khan Shaykhun attacks were not perpetrated by Syrian troops, who was behind them? Carla del Ponte, a former member of the Independent International Commission of Inquiry on the Syrian Arab Republic, may have shown us a path in May 2013 when she referred to other chemical attacks that had taken place that spring. "We still have to deepen our investigation, verify and confirm [the findings] through new witness testimony, but according to what we have established so far, it is at the moment opponents of the regime who are using sarin gas", she had stated in an interview on the Swiss radio. The following day, in a reaction to Del Ponte's comments, the Independent International Commission had issued a press release clarifying that it "[had] not reached conclusive findings as to the use of chemical weapons in Syria by any parties in the conflict." It was predictable that Del Ponte would be slandered for her comments, as she had previously been when she had claimed in a book that the Kosovo Albanians had smuggled human organs of kidnapped Serbs after the Kosovo war ended in 1999. The International Criminal Tribunal for the former Yugoslavia had taken issue with her views, stating that there was "no evidence in support of such allegations." Yet, according to a draft report from the Council of Europe cited by *The Daily Telegraph*, Kosovar Prime Minister Hashim Thaci was one of the key players in the traffic of organs of Serb prisoners after the 1998-99 conflict.

Now, let's ask this question: did the rebels possess sarin? Most likely. An *Associated Press* reporter got hold of an audio recording involving an ISIS militant who boasted of getting sarin from Saudi Arabian intelligence agents. Saudi Arabia reportedly provided funds for the purchase of the toxic products through the staff of one of its embassies. Which one? We may have half an answer: another journalist, Yahya Ababneh, collected statements from witnesses in Goutha who confirmed that rebels had received chemical weapons from Saudi Arabia through the head of the intelligence bureau, the famous Prince Bandar bin Sultan, also former Saudi Ambassador to Washington. Here is our man back to the forefront of the Islamic scene. These "pro-Saudi" rebels are believed to be responsible for the August 21, 2013, sarin attack, according to Yahya Ababneh. Sarin is no stranger to Saudi Arabia as it has used it in its war against the Houthis in Yemen, including in Sanaa on August 25, 2016, according to a Yemeni military source, an attack that left many dead and wounded in the ninth district of the capital. In Aleppo, Syria, *CNN* reporter Frederik Pleitgen discovered chemicals in a factory located in the Masaken Hanano District, an area controlled by terrorists. If we rely on Seymour Hersh, British and American services had known since at least spring 2013 that rebels possessed chemical weapons, just as they knew that the Turks and the Saudis were their main suppliers. In May 2015, a dozen men from the Al-Nusra Front were arrested in southern Turkey while in possession of about four pounds of equipment used in the production of sarin. Most of those men were released without charge. Their leader, the Syrian Haytham Qassab, was sentenced *in absentia* to 12 years in prison. A classified document from the U.S. National Ground Intelligence Center confirmed that Al-Nusra was itself in possession of sarin gas. Suburbs of Damascus were hit by rockets containing sarin in August 2013, around the same time as the attack on Goutha that the West attributed to the Syrian government. A UN mission had also investigated the series of chemical attacks perpetrated in Syria in March and April 2013. Seymour Hersh quoted a source within that mission who told him that the first attack, that of March 19 in Khan al-Assal, a village near Aleppo, was the work of the rebels; nineteen civilians and one Syrian soldier had been killed, while several had been injured. Members of the UN team had interviewed witnesses, including doctors who had treated the victims, and all had stated that gas had been used in the attack. The mainstream media had remained silent on the matter, but *Mint Press News* had revealed the existence of an arms cache in a building in Aleppo, which was used for the storage of chemical weapons intended for the 16th infantry division of the

Free Syrian Army (FSA). But the FSA, ISIS and the Al-Nusra Front were not the only organizations competing in the chemical weapons race. Zahran Alloush, ex-commander of Jaysh al-Islam, had obtained 1,100 pounds of sarin gas and cyanide from the Turkish intelligence. In this regard, two members of the Kurdish parliament, Eren Erdem and Ali Seker, had made an inflammatory statement at a press conference in October 2015, saying that they had records proving that the Turkish government had supplied sarin gas to the Islamic State, which has used it against civilians. So, once again we find the Turkish government in the picture. It is actually a fortunate coincidence because another assumption has been proposed for the Ghouta attacks: the Erdogan government allegedly wished to spark off an American intervention as part of a "false flag operation", meaning that Syria would have been blamed for a strike launched by the Turkish forces. Ankara, for that matter, is said to have planned to carry out this type of operation on the other side of the border, in Syria, where the tomb of Suleyman Shah is located, near Aleppo, a place under the property of Turkey. Had Erdogan succeeded in this project, his American counterpart, Barack Obama, would have had no choice but to declare that al-Assad had crossed the "red line" by using chemical weapons. That is at least what the Turkish despot thought.

The Red line. The formula came precisely right out of Obama's mouth on August 20, 2012, when the former president warned the Syrian government against the use of chemical weapons. The irony was that a year almost to the day after Obama's statement occurred the tragic events of Goutha. At the time, the head of the White House was ready to send ground troops to Syria, but he did not do so, which made Erdogan angry. As a final step, Obama accepted al-Assad's proposal to relinquish his chemical arsenal as part of a negotiated agreement with Russia. But unofficially, the decision not to intervene in Syria was due, according to Seymour Hersh, to the Pentagon's reluctance, the five-star generals questioning the legitimacy of the intervention. American Army officers were made aware, thanks to information obtained by the Defense Intelligence Agency (DIA), that it was Turkey, not Syria, that was behind the Goutha attacks. The Pentagon had gathered evidence about this matter through analyses performed at the British government laboratory in Porton Down, UK, after Russian military intelligence officers collected sarin samples in Goutha. The analyses revealed that the toxic compound did not match the one the Syrian regime possessed. The results were communicated to the U.S. Chairman of the Joint Chiefs of Staff and then to the President himself.

Hersch's thesis is interesting and deserves a closer look, but the thing is that recent analyses conducted by other laboratories, which worked for the Organization for the Prohibition of Chemical Weapons (OPCW), substantiated the Syrian regime's involvement in the main chemical attacks since 2013. The samples came from Goutha, Khan al-Assal, and Khan Shaykhun. The tests also showed that two compounds of the sample collected in Ghouta matched those found in Khan Shaykhun. So, what should we conclude? That the Syrian regime was primarily responsible for the chemical attacks, but that it was not the only one to possess chemical weapons, some of which seem to have been supplied to the rebels by countries allied to the United States, including Turkey and, of course, Saudi Arabia.

Financing ISIS

On June 28, 2018, LafargeHolcim, a world leader in building materials, was charged with "complicity in crimes against humanity", "financing terrorists", "endangering the lives" of its employees, and "breaking an embargo." What for? Because the Swiss company bribed jihadist groups to keep its Syrian factory in operation. In 2011, shortly after the start of the civil war in Syria, various insurgent groups began to deploy in the vicinity of the factory operated by Lafarge, located in north-central Syria, a few miles from the Turkish-Syrian border. But unlike other companies, Lafarge never agreed to close down its Syrian business. There was, then, only one option left: convince the insurgents to maintain the factory open by offering them money in return for a promise to stay away from the area. It was *Le Monde* newspaper that had disclosed the details of this case in June 2016, which had prompted the Paris prosecutor's office to launch a preliminary investigation in October that year. A complaint was finally filed by the French Ministry of Finance and an official investigation opened in June 2017. Lafarge, therefore, indirectly financed terrorist activities for purely commercial reasons, but there was more: the company allegedly gave false financial statements and accounting records to the French government in order to conceal the bribes it had paid to the insurgents.

Lafarge-Holcim was formed in 2015 by a merger of Lafarge, based in France, and Holcim, a Swiss company. It has 80,000 employees in nearly 80 countries. For a time, it handed over about $100,000 each month to armed groups, including the Al-Qaeda-affiliated Al-Nusra Front and the Islamic State, the latter receiving alone more than $20,000 as a monthly payment. In all, ISIS collected $509,694 from the Syrian subsidiary of the Lafarge group. These payments extended over two years, from July 2012 to September 2014. A total of $15.5 million was allegedly paid by the company to jihadist factions in Syria. Lafarge's foray into this country precedes the merger with Holcim and dates back to the end of 2007 when its ex-CEO, Bruno Lafont, signed a contract worth €8.8 billion to buy the Egyptian group Orascom, which was dominating the cement sector in the Middle East and Africa with ten factories in Egypt, Saudi Arabia, Nigeria, South Africa and Turkey. The firm was headed by Nassef Sawiris, one of Egypt's richest men. Under the terms of the transaction concluded between Lafarge and Orascom, Sawiris obtained an 11.4% stake in Lafarge and a seat on its board of directors. At the time, an Orascom project had received little attention: building a state-of-the-art facility in northern Syria. Sawiris had long coveted that country, which he saw as an untapped market characterized by a growing economy. The idea of building a $680 million factory near Jalabiya, a desolate tract of land about 60 miles northwest of Raqqa and not far from the Turkish border, sprang up in 2006 in the businessman's mind. But for the factory to be built, Sawiris needed a local partner capable of navigating through the Syrian bureaucracy and gaining the support of President Bashar al-Assad. That local partner was Firas Tlass, an influential businessman close to the regime. Tlass agreed to play the role of a "broker" for the Jalabiya project in exchange for a 1.3% ownership share with an option for an acquisition that could go up to 10%, plus a 1% payment of the plant's annual revenues. Sawiris gave him a positive response and the construction of the factory began as planned. But those great moments were soon relegated to history in 2012 as unrest erupted in the factory's surrounding areas. Rebel groups began setting up checkpoints on all the roads leading to the facility, demanding bribes and harassing Lafarge workers. In August 2012, Nidal Wahbi, the factory's human resources manager, was kidnapped in Manbij by five gunmen belonging to a branch of the Free Syrian Army. The kidnappers demanded $200,000, but Jacob Waerness, Lafarge's security chief in Syria, refused to pay the ransom, believing that such a move would only encourage hostage-taking. Wahbi was detained for three days before he managed to come up with $20,000 from relatives, which apparently was enough to buy his release. The only downside was that when he asked Lafarge to repay the ransom, the company turned him down. Ironically, two months later, nine workers were taken hostage while driving in a van near Raqqa. This time, Lafarge paid the required ransom, $200,000.

With time, Firas Tlass turned away from the al-Assad government and became a major sponsor to various rebel groups aligned to the West. Responding to an invitation from Bruno Pescheux, the Jalabiya factory's manager, Tlass agreed to act as an intermediary between the company and the rebels for a bribe of $75,000 a month. Pescheux had no choice but to accept the terms. One of Tlass's first steps was to draw up a list of groups that Lafarge needed to buy off in order to allow employees to get through checkpoints and secure supplies. The list included eighteen groups, ranging from the People's Protection Unit of Kurdistan, or YPG, to the "Manbij Council", the "Euphrates Bridge Checkpoint", the "Aleppo People", and the Free Syrian Army. Even if, initially, the list baffled Bruno Pescheux, he nevertheless handed over the money to those obscure organizations. Court documents show that the manager did everything to conceal the details of the payments. Most of those payments were made through a personal bank account that Pescheux had created for the occasion. An internal investigation conducted in 2017 by PricewaterhouseCoopers found that the Syrian factory used a total of 54 bank accounts in the Middle East to transfer money to Tlass via Pescheux's account in order "to protect the anonymity of the [Lafarge] staff member processing the transactions." Pescheux ultimately decided to spill the beans; he admitted that the company was paying up to $140,000 a month to the rebels. And all the payments went through Firas Tlass, who is the one to whom Lafarge was sending the "protection dollars" every month. But Lafarge Cement Syria also paid ransoms for the release of a few hostages of the Alawite faith, a service rendered to the Syrian government. Documents show that Firas Tlass received a total of $5.4 million between July 2012 and August 2014 as an exchange of favors.

In 2013, the factory's production started to decline. In the summer of 2014, relations between the facility's management and at least one group, namely the Islamic State, reached a breaking point. So much so that Bruno Pescheux settled on terminating the cement plant's activities in July. A few weeks later, the French manager was transferred to another Lafarge subsidiary in Africa. His successor, Frédéric Jolibois, felt confident enough to resume business activities in August. A resumption that was short-lived, though, because in September the Islamic State defeated the Kurds in Kobani, a city located about 31 miles from the factory, which was finally stormed by the jihadist group on September 19. An evacuation plan had been devised for the employees, the company's spokespersons said, but it was probably never put in place because the poor workers had to hide in the factory tunnels to avoid being crushed by the jihadists. On December 22, 2014, a shady character by the name of Amro Taleb, a Syrian-Canadian, met Abu Luqman, governor of the Islamic State in the province of Aleppo, to discuss "business." This Abu Luqman, who was also ISIS's intelligence chief, was not a newcomer. He had been closely involved, according to *Liberation* newspaper, "in the terror campaign in Europe, and probably in the attacks of November 13, 2015, in France, as well as that of March 22, 2016, in Brussels." He was reportedly killed by an Iraqi airstrike on April 17, 2018. As for Amro Taleb, his role was unclear. Owner of an import-export company based in Turkey, near the Syrian border, Taleb claimed to be an environmental management consultant for the

Syrian government and Lafarge. What we know about him, though, is that he and two members of the Jalabiya factory's management, that is, Mamdouh al-Khaled, the "production manager", and Ahmad Jamal, the "main supplier", defrauded the company through some kind of ploy. At the end of the game, an agreement was reached between Lafarge and the Islamic State: the Swiss company would sell the factory to the jihadist group so it could resume the production. But the *Charlie Hebdo* shooting in January 2015 ultimately convinced Lafarge against reaching any deal with ISIS. A year later, the company had no choice but to write off its investment in Syria.

Lafarge's questionable business practices in that country were just an extension of the underground activities it had carried out in Iraq years earlier. Marianne Gasior, a whistleblower and former attorney for Kennametal, a supplier of tooling and industrial materials, said that Lafarge once provided "turnkey" services to Saddam Hussein's arms export network. The Swiss company owns—or used to own—2,600 acres of land on the Marblehead Peninsula, Ohio, where it houses—or used to house—an ammunition factory known simply as the "Ordnance Center". Gasior claimed that the CIA used the property as a transshipment spot for clandestine deliveries of arms and military equipment to Iraq during the 1980s, and possibly even after the coming into effect of the American embargo put in place on August 5, 1990. From Marblehead, the equipment, Gasior alleges, was carried on cargo ships along the St. Lawrence River, in Canada, up to the United Kingdom where Kennametal's subsidiary relabeled some of the goods as manufactured on the European continent. Everything was ultimately exported to Iraq. These shipments, said Gasior, never drew the attention of U.S. border controls, the CIA ensuring immunity to the crews. When the case was leaked out, the Justice Department was asked to bury the investigation, again according to Gasior. Because of the CIA? Probably, but perhaps also because one well-known lady, Hillary Clinton, was a member of the Lafarge's Board of directors from 1990 to 1992, and because Lafarge was one of Clinton's clients when she did legal work for the company through Rose Law Firm in Little Rock, Arkansas. With her husband soon to be in the driver's seat in Washington, Hillary Clinton couldn't afford to take any risks. It is important to note, though, that Marianne Gasior's statements have not been corroborated by any mainstream media.

Other players did business with ISIS. During its best days, the group's primary sources of revenue came from taxation, extortion, robbery of economic assets, kidnapping for ransom, donations from Saudi Arabia and other Gulf states, often disguised as "humanitarian charity", material support from foreign fighters, online fundraising, but most of all, oil traffic. The black gold was sold illegally in Turkey and generated between one and three million dollars a day, depending on various estimates. At the height of its glory, ISIS controlled 300 oil wells in Iraq and 60% of Syria's oil capacity. And according to Iraqi officials, if the Kurds initially blocked ISIS's oil trade, they quickly smelled the money and later joined the jihadist group in its criminal entreprise. The Kurdistan Democratic Party, the Patriotic Union of Kurdistan and the Peshmerga have greatly benefited from the transport of oil through the Kurdish territory. Trucks belonging to Meersoma, a Nokan Group's front company run by the Patriotic Union of Kurdistan, got its supply from an oil refinery itself supplied by the Taq Taq oil field, in the Kurdistan Region of Iraq, which can produce up to 215,000 barrels per day. The product was then sent to Kurdish organizations in Kirkuk. The Turkish government is said to have turned a blind eye to this traffic, which might explain why the smuggled oil transited through the port of Ceyhan, Turkey. Within the Islamic State, the man who oversaw the administration of everything concerning the gas and oil industry was one Abu Sayyaf. Sayyaf had built up a network of traders and wholesalers that enabled the Islamist organization to triple its revenues. He was also the one who approved expenditures in other areas such as the management of the slave market as well as the reconstruction and repair of facilities that had suffered damage caused by the bombings. On May 15, 2015, members of the U.S. Delta Force, a detachment of the Joint Special Operations Command in Iraq, were deployed to capture Sayyaf in Al-Amr, Syria. He and a dozen other ISIS fighters died during the operation that resulted in the release of Yazidi slaves. Nineteen other jihadists were killed in the air raids that followed. In Abu Sayyaf's lair, the U.S. troops recovered documents containing crucial information that helped to better understand ISIS's structure. It was thus learned that the organization's revenues in the six months preceding February 2015 had been $289.5 million. Abu Sayyaf's activities alone accounted for 72% of the jihadist group's revenues.

ISIS Fighters Evacuated Thanks to Uncle Sam and Uncle Brit

The news hit the media head-on in the fall of 2017: the United States and the United Kingdom allowed hundreds of ISIS fighters to evacuate Raqqa, Syria, with impunity. The information was reported by the *BBC* in November, but a few second-class media had preceded the British network as early as October. The deal was concluded with a local council made up of Kurdish and Arab tribal leaders, who said they had appealed to the coalition and the Syrian Democratic Forces (SDF, a coalition of Arabs and Kurds) to allow the evacuation of local ISIS fighters in order to curb the violence in Raqqa. The coalition, however, quickly set the record straight, stating that it had not been involved in the discussions that had led to this agreement, but that it believed the move had saved innocent lives. Oddly enough, the Americans had made it clear from the start that only a surrender would be acceptable, not a simple negotiated withdrawal. The main U.S. envoy to the coalition, Brett McGurk, had gone so far as to say that foreign fighters in Raqqa were all going to "die in battle." The future proved him wrong. The United States, it seems, does not fear paradoxes as it had strongly opposed a previous agreement negotiated by Hezbollah aimed at evacuating ISIS fighters to Iraq, whose roads were constantly bombed by American jet fighters; these had finally had to cease the operations under the pressure from the Russians.

If the Raqqa evacuation was brought to light, it was certainly not because of the SDF, since they had blocked access to the city, even preventing the media from entering it. Flooded with questions, the leaders of the organization finally admitted to authorizing the evacuation, but added that it had involved only a few dozen combatants. Yet, that is not what the *BBC* found out. According to one of the truck drivers who transported the fighters and who was quoted by the British network, as many as about 4,000 people, combatants and civilians, were part of the convoy that stretched over three or four miles and included some "50 trucks, 13 buses and more than 100 of the Islamic State's […] vehicles." Ten trucks were loaded with weapons and ammunition. A very large number of those combatants were foreigners, some of whom even came from France. Did they return to their country? Hard to say, but according to the Turkish President Recep Tayyip Erdogan, all those jihadists and their families went to Egypt to wage an armed struggle in the Sinai Peninsula. An SDF member told the *Jerusalem Post* that some of the civilians had been used as human shields, the ISIS fighters wishing to avoid airstrikes. These had even taken their Yazidi slaves with them during the three-day journey. In September 2018, *Press-TV* revealed details of another case with a similar outline: U.S. transport aircraft evacuated four members of the Islamic State to the eastern province of Deir ez-Zor, Syria. The Syrian Observatory for Human Rights had raised the matter in August 2017, but the information could not be corroborated by any media outlet.

One cannot fail to draw a comparison between the events revealed above and another aberration of history, the *Kunduz airlift*, or the "airlift of evil." An aberration that some described as unjustifiable and that occurred between November 14 and 25, 2001, from Kunduz, Afghanistan. In the aftermath of 9/11, if the main Al-Qaeda and Taliban leaders' escape had gone well to some extent, the same was not true in Kunduz, a city of nearly 300,000 inhabitants where several of these combatants had been surrounded by the coalition forces. But at President Pervez Musharraf's request, they were allowed to flee. And there were many of them: Taliban fighters and members of Al-Qaeda but also Chechens, jihadists from Russia and China, and even young students from Pakistan's Koranic schools who were there to assist the Taliban at the invitation of their imams. There were even Pakistanis from the United Kingdom who had no qualms about betraying their host country. But above all, there was an impressive number of agents from the

Inter-Services Intelligence (ISI), Pakistan's premier intelligence agency, which were also on-site to help the Taliban in their fight against the American forces and the Northern Alliance. Thus, pressured by Musharraf, the United States thought it wise to allow the evacuation of this collection of obscurantists, and this, even though they were sworn enemies of America, having wiped 3,000 of its citizens off the map. The Pakistani President had managed to win American support by warning the White House that losing hundreds and perhaps thousands of men in Kunduz would be embarrassing and would jeopardize his political survival. Dozens of senior Pakistani military officers, including two generals, were then airlifted to Pakistan, in addition to the ISI agents. The Musharraf government had dispatched around 50 trucks and helicopters to transport the besieged, while battalions of Pakistani soldiers controlled the airport.

Washington and Islamabad denied that the event ever occurred. When journalists asked Donald Rumsfeld about it, the Secretary of Defense's response was, "neither Pakistan nor any other country flew any planes into Afghanistan to evacuate anybody." It was a lie. During the siege, the leaders of the Northern Alliance had stated that they were going to treat foreign fighters, which included Pakistani military advisers and Arab volunteers, more severely than their Afghan counterparts. It was some sort of revenge after the Taliban and some of their Arab allies had committed mass killings against Afghan civilians who had dared to support the Northern Alliance. According to author and journalist Ahmed Rashid, it was Dick Cheney who had ordered the Kunduz airlift, with Donald Rumsfeld not too far behind. And the decision to allow the evacuation was made without the main secretaries' knowledge, among them Colin Powell, who was made aware of it a few days after the end of the operations. Planes and helicopters had taken off from bases in Chitral and Gilgit, Pakistan, to land in Kunduz under the watchful eye of members of the United States Army Special Forces, frustrated to see the enemy running away so easily. If we are to believe an Indian intelligence source, about 8,000 men had been trapped inside Kunduz during the final days of the siege, roughly half of them from Pakistan. The Indians estimated that 3,300 prisoners were left to a tribal faction led by General Abdul Rashid Dostum of the Northern Alliance, while several hundred Taliban were turned over to tribal leaders. If we do the math, that leaves over 4,000 men evacuated by the airlift.

"I'll See You Guys in New York"

On the night of October 26 to 27, 2019, the United States launched *Operation Kayla Mueller* to carry on with a mission that began on June 7, 2006, with the killing of Abu Musab al-Zarqawi, the former Al-Qaeda leader in Iraq. But that time, though, the target was Abu Bakr al-Baghdadi, the self-proclaimed "caliph" of the Islamic State. The operation took place in the outskirts of the city of Barisha, in the governorate of Idlib, Syria, and was conducted in conformity with the best practices, without causing too much "collateral damage." According to General Kenneth McKenzie, head of the United States Central Command (CENTCOM) who oversaw the operation, Baghdadi committed suicide and killed two children when he detonated his belt while trying to escape from the American forces. Thus, after al-Zarqawi and Osama bin Laden, the United States had just gotten rid of the world's third best known jihadist. But how did the Americans manage to track down a man whose intentions no one suspected a few years ago? The answer has nothing to surprise the reader: what led to the October 2019 operation is a series of mistakes and misjudgments for which Iraqis, Syrians, Yazidis and even Westerners have paid dearly.

One cannot explain the rise of the thug who spread terror in the Middle East without addressing the heart of the problem: the American intervention in Iraq. At that time, al-Baghdadi was attending the University of Baghdad, but when the United States started to rain bombs down on his country, he vowed revenge, like thousands of other Iraqis. He then set out to put on the jihadist uniform, and after the first American assaults in 2003, the future head of ISIS was among the founders of the Jamaat Jaysh Ahl al-Sunnah wa-l-Jamaah, in which he presided the sharia committee. But not for a long time, as he was arrested in early February 2004 by the occupying forces and detained first in the infamous Abu Ghraib prison, then at Camp Bucca as a "civilian detainee" in a medium-security compound. Some suggest that he was released in December 2004, but most reports lean more toward 2009. In the meantime, the Islamic law, the sharia, was the ruling authority inside Camp Bucca, which could accommodate no less than 25,000 prisoners. As a consequence, the Islamists, and only them, were calling the shots and leading the herd within the prison walls. For the U.S. military who guarded the premises, Bucca had become a "training ground for Islamic extremism", contributing to the rise of the Islamic State. A total of nine members of ISIS's high command spent time in Bucca, not counting militants of lesser importance. Al-Baghdadi, on his side, was seen among his jailers as a sort of "fixer", that is, an arbitrator or a mediator, therefore a man who could be trusted. But most of all, he was nothing like the fighter the world would see in action years later. His stay in prison, however, changed the rules of the game. Despite the radicalization and re-education programs set up by the Americans, many men in Bucca, including al-Baghdadi himself, became true time bombs overnight. Former detainees told the *Al Jazeera* network that the camp was nothing less than an "Al-Qaeda school", where extremists were even able to offer lessons on explosives and suicide bombing techniques. A former prisoner, Adel Jasim Mohammed, said that the U.S. military staff was doing nothing to prevent the radicals from indoctrinating other detainees. No wonder the deradicalization programs were nothing but complete fiascos. In 2009, the future ISIS's leader was finally released. That day, he may have intended to pitch a bad joke when he told his jailers: "I'll see you guys in New York." It appears that none of those jailers, many of whom were part of the 306 Military Police Battalion, a unit based on Long Island, saw a threat in this "joke." It was a serious mistake because that year, hundreds, if not thousands, were released before, at the same time, or after al-Baghdadi, and several subsequently formed the bulk of what would become the Islamic State. To explain this series of releases that would haunt the hallways of Western chancelleries for a decade, the Republicans quickly searched for a fall guy. This fall guy was, obviously, Barack Obama. But those Republicans were way off the beam because the man behind the release of al-Baghdadi and his cronies was none other than George W. Bush. In

2008, Bush, willing to reduce the number of American soldiers in Iraq, signed an agreement with Baghdad that required that all the detainees be handed over to the Iraqi forces. According to this agreement, al-Baghdadi was transferred to Iraqi custody in 2009 and released a little later for unclear reasons. Little by little, the Islamic State would climb the ladder and become the most important jihadist group since the best years of Al-Qaeda. In an ultimate twist of fate, on June 29, 2014, al-Baghdadi announced the establishment of a worldwide caliphate and proclaimed himself "commander of the faithful", as Mullah Omar of the Taliban had done years before. So much for the clarification.

It was at that moment that the hunt for al-Baghdadi began for the Americans, a hunt that ended in October 2019. Among those who helped find the former ISIS leader are the Syrian Democratic Forces (SDF). Before the raid, the SDF, in conjunction with the U.S. government, had spent five months gathering information on al-Baghdadi, even succeeding in attracting an ISIS defector who had provided critical information on the leader's whereabouts. An SDF commander, Mazloum Abdi, said that their informant was part of al-Baghdadi's inner circle as a security adviser, which is why he was able to give a detailed plan of the Barisha compound. The Americans realized that this informant was a trusted man when he gave them a pair of the leader's underwear and a sample of his blood. The subsequent DNA analyzes proved to be positive, which confirmed the presence of al-Baghdadi in Barisha. A woman named Nisrine Assad Ibrahim also helped the Americans track down the ISIS's strongman, at least for a time. Captured in Syria by a Delta Forces unit, Ibrahim was accused of being involved in some of the Islamic State's most heinous crimes; she was sentenced to death by a court in Erbil, Iraq. Despite this tragic fate, she agreed to cooperate with the authorities. In February 2016, she identified a house in Mosul where al-Baghdadi was staying, but the United States refrained from carrying out an airstrike, fearing that it might cause civilian casualties in the densely packed neighborhood. The hunt went on for a while until the D-day in October 2019. And at least one country, namely Turkey, boasted of having been much of a help in that hunt, although no one knows precisely how this help was provided—assuming there was any help. An American official, whose name has not been disclosed, said that Turkey had been informed about the operation before the attack, but not about the target due to concerns in Washington that the information would become compromised. After all, many questioned the intentions of the Turks, knowing that al-Baghdadi had taken refuge in a town 23 miles from the Turkish-Syrian border. Brett McGurk, a former United States envoy for the anti-Islamic State coalition, wrote in a *Washington Post* column: "It is telling that the U.S. military reportedly chose to launch this operation from hundreds of miles away in Iraq, as opposed to facilities in Turkey, a NATO ally, just across the border." It was known that one of al-Baghdadi's brothers traveled to Istanbul several times as a courier since the end of 2018, delivering messages to and from ISIS operatives, according to Iraqi intelligence officials. No one knows who the brother met in the Turkish capital, and what were his meetings all about.

EPILOGUE

The Free Syrian Army (FSA) has been at the heart of the Syrian conflict, and the US-led coalition relied on it, at least initially, to eject Bashar al-Assad from his seat. But experts and observers quickly realized in the aftermath of the Arab Spring that the FSA was some sort of a "UMO", an "unidentified military object." Many reports have spoken of an army half-full of jihadists, others have alluded to its disappearance in 2015. We know at least one thing, that the FSA was operating into murky waters throughout the course. Large figures of fundamentalist Islam supported the organization from the outset: Qatar, Saudi Arabia, Turkey, and even the Al-Nusra Front in certain circumstances. That so-called army, deep down, followed in the footsteps of other Western allies that worshipped the devil rather than his opposite. The mujahideen, Saddam Hussein in the eighties, the Kosovar militias close to Al-Qaeda: the United States has this tendency to walk alongside the worst thugs. "Thugs" being a term that suits well to the FSA members, who were accused several times of violating human rights and fundamental freedoms. It was, for all of us, easier to think that America had learned lessons from the Afghan adventure and its consequences, the attacks of September 11, 2001. The mujahideen, who were given hundreds of millions of dollars by Uncle Sam, turned their backs to their sponsor fifteen years later to bring down buildings that, until then, had been the greatest symbol of modern capitalism. As an act of revenge, the United States shelled Iraq for years, even though this country had nothing to do with 9/11. Then, it was Libya's turn to undergo surgery to remove the Gaddafi regime, a feat that could not be repeated in Syria. But each time, the coalition, made up largely of Western countries, was assisted on the ground by troops full of fundamentalists.

Here is an excerpt from an article written by journalist James Harkin, which appeared in *Vanity Fair*. In *Evaporated in Syria, the Most Dangerous Place in the World*, Harkin talks about the kidnapping of James Foley and other journalists in Syrian territory. After reading, we get to know more about the Free Syrian Army in all its "splendor."

I first got the details of Jim Foley's kidnapping, a month after it happened, by way of a Syrian who goes by "Yasser." I had known Yasser before the uprising, and he has been involved with the revolt from the beginning. He and his Free Syrian Army colleagues were working on the assumption that Foley had been driven to a nearby Shiite village, called Fua, by pro-regime shabiha—the ruthless militias who do so much of Assad's dirty work—and then dispatched hundreds of kilometers south [of] Damascus. Some while later, in May 2013, GlobalPost, one of the news organizations Foley had worked for, advanced much the same scenario. Relying on "multiple independent reports from very credible confidential sources," GlobalPost reported that Foley was being held in a Damascus prison run by Syrian Air Force Intelligence, the most feared arm of the shadowy Syrian security state, along with at least one other Western journalist, probably another American—possibly Austin Tice. The investigation was the work of Kroll, a firm of private security contractors that GlobalPost had hired at considerable expense.

[...]

The theory that Jim Foley was abducted by pro-regime shabiha, however, a theory propounded by Yasser and endorsed by the GlobalPost, makes very little sense. Foley was traveling from the rebel stronghold of Binnish en route to a rebel border crossing called Bab al-Hawa; the whole point of that circuitous route was to avoid the regime-held outpost of Fua and the attention of the shabiha. Six months earlier the area would have been thick with regime agents, but now both Fua and Taftanaz airport were under siege by Syrian rebels and wild-eyed foreign jihadis. In extensive interviews with journalists who have worked the area and know it well, I talked to no one who had any enthusiasm for the theory that Foley could have been spirited away to Fua. (The Assad regime has denied having Foley in its custody.)

[...]

The term [shabiha] is nearly 30 years old and originally referred to gangs of smugglers along Syria's borders whose regime connections gave them license to do as they pleased. Since the outbreak of the uprising, many have simply transferred their loyalties to the fledgling Free Syrian Army and set about smuggling arms. For some of these gangs, kidnapping for ransom is a way of life; war-ravaged Syria has made it a flourishing business. In March 2013 the BBC's well-known world-affairs correspondent, Paul Wood, was traveling in Syria with a group of rebel-friendly smugglers when he and three colleagues were abducted by masked gunmen at a checkpoint. They were held for 10 days in a tiny concrete cell under one of the smugglers' homes; it ended only when they overpowered a guard and forced their way out. The kidnappers had started by claiming they were regime-affiliated shabiha; it soon became clear that they were a criminal gang flying the flag of the Free Syrian Army and working closely with Islamic extremists.

[...]

In the early stages of the conflict, Syria's rebel armies had been happy to protect visiting journalists with their lives; if the world could only see the iniquities of the Syrian regime, the rebels thought, the Western powers would be shamed into [a] large-scale military intervention on their behalf. When that didn't happen, some of them found a more creative use for the journalists slipping into Syria—as commodities to be traded for cash.

[...]

A month after Paul Wood's kidnapping, an Italian reporter named Domenico Quirico and a Belgian teacher named Pierre Piccinin da Prata were traveling together near the city of Al-Qusayr when they were taken by bandits working for a large rebel militia called the Farouq Brigade; it took five months and a considerable ransom to get them out. (In an interview on the Syrian-Turkish border, a well-connected rebel from Al-Qusayr told me that the ransom for the pair was around $5 million, $4 million of which seems to have come from the Italian government.) Two weeks after that a French-American photographer named Jonathan Alpeyrie was likely betrayed by a fixer soon after he crossed the Lebanese border into Syria; nearly three months and several mock executions later, he was released after $450,000 was paid by a pro-regime businessman to his Free Syrian Army kidnappers.

Thank you for buying this book!

Please, feel free to share your comments about the book.

You can also visit the author's personal website at https://ericpilon.com, where a great many articles expose the establishment's abuses of power, or this website, https://medium.com/black-list, where the author challenges mainstream media's narratives and debunks fake news.

www.ingramcontent.com/pod-product-compliance
Lightning Source LLC
Chambersburg PA
CBHW071421150726
48000CB00001B/428